AF449861

ISBN 978-88-8398-085-5
Copyright © 2019 by European Press Academic Publishing
Florence, Italy
www.e-p-a-p.com
www.europeanpress.eu
Proprietà letteraria riservata—Printed in Italy, UK and USA

Working methods of
the European Parliament
Administration
in Multi-actors World
A case-study

Giancarlo Vilella

EUROPEAN PRESS ACADEMIC PUBLISHING

Florence, Italy

**European Parliament Fellowship 2018-2019
at the European University Institute (EUI), Florence**

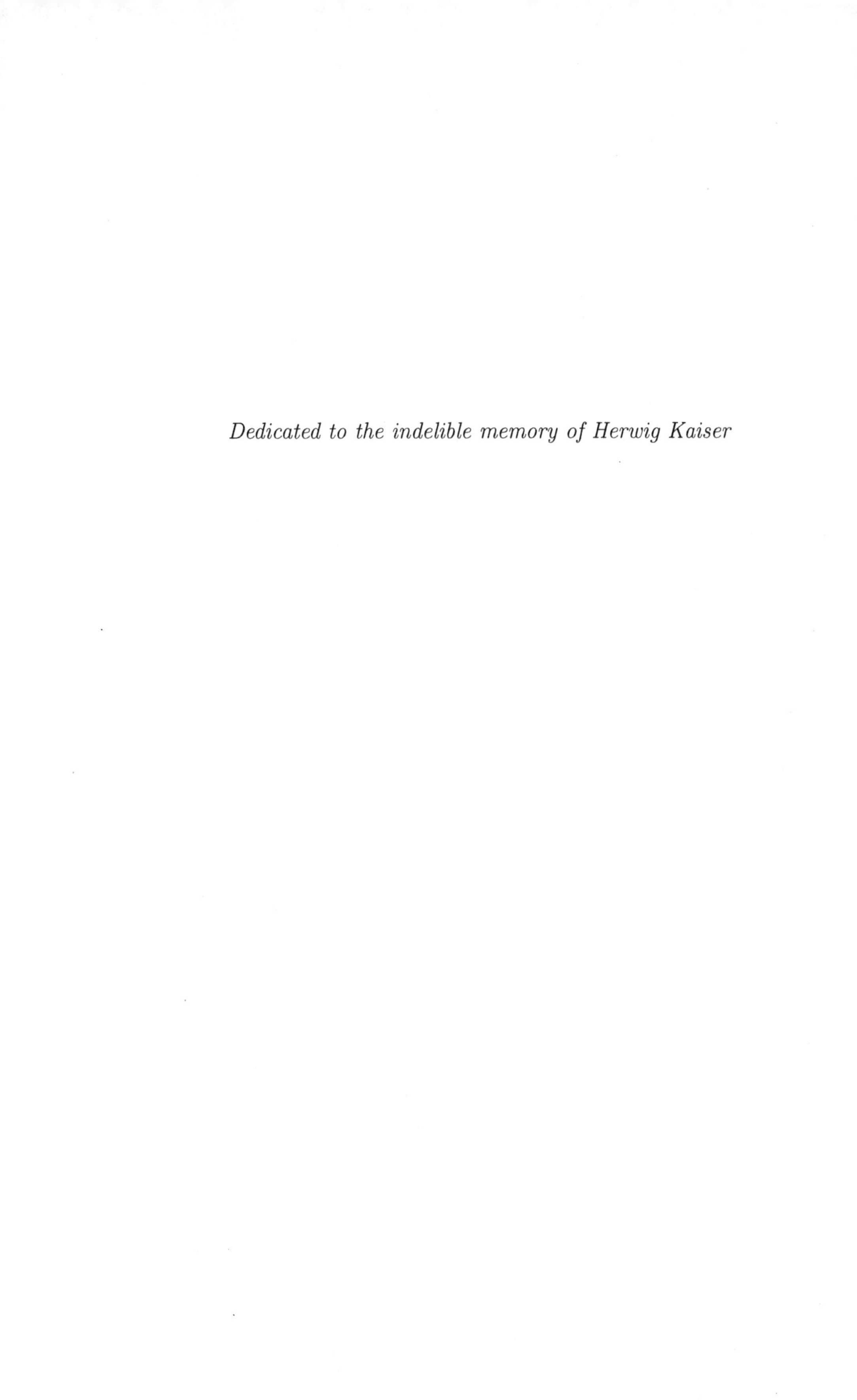

Dedicated to the indelible memory of Herwig Kaiser

Foreword

by Vincenzo Grassi
Secretary General of the European University Institute (Florence)

"I have seen things you people wouldn't believe". It is one of the most famous quotes in the history of film, and at the time of writing on the day of charismatic actor Rutger Hauer's passing, it is one that provides a timely source of inspiration for this preface. In *Blade Runner*, Roy Batty may have been talking of attack ships on fire and C-beams glittering in the dark, but unprecedented migration flows, climate change denying, economic austerity and menacing union disintegration hauntingly make credible substitutes.

As Giancarlo Vilella clearly indicates, the European Union is facing challenges. Blinded by their conviction and passion for the European project, such challenges were unfathomable to the likes of Robert Schuman, Alcide De Gasperi or Jean Monnet. Moreover, they are challenges that were equally unpredictable even for key players in the most recent decades while European integration pushed into the creation of an ever-closer union and a single currency.

An original approach alongside rigorous methodology make this concise, yet profound, book a highly significant contribution to the study of the European Parliament's political and administrative role in facing the current crisis. It does so by addressing those well-established notions that until very recently have been shaping international relationships: democracy, multilateralism, European integration.

This year's European elections throw a spotlight on the extent of fractures and divisions that have come to riddle the European integration project. The European Union and its member states are now confronted with different philosophical visions even on the rule of law and the fundamental values enshrined in the Lisbon Treaty. These new fractures mingle with more traditional divergences between 'rich' versus 'less wealthy', 'North' versus 'South', 'guardians of a strict budgetary discipline' versus 'supporters of risk-sharing'.

A rise in populism may be casting a threatening shadow over the Union, encouraging heightened Euroscepticism. But a majority of European citizens still holds on to a perception that the key to facing the increasing number of transnational challenges lies in investing in a project that promotes shared prosperity and peace. That said, citizens' patience is being tested. Recent events have dented the European Commission's credibility as an independent supranational power, and the Council has been unsuccessful in identifying effective and timely solutions to fight poverty and social inequality within Europe, and to manage migration flows. European citizens' waning belief in these two institutions paves a way for the European Parliament to step up to centre stage on the institutional scene.

Institutional developments, such as attributing the European Parliament with the right of legislative initiative, are pushed up the agenda. Here, Vilella emphasises an opportunity for the Parliament to take important actions in administrative areas to reduce the gap between European citizens and the European institutional system. Several of the proposals discussed appear as mere organisational and procedural steps, but which have the potential to make the exercise of parliamentary responsibility more transparent and its accountability more visible to its citizens.

In previous works, the author has contributed extensively to the crucial issue of e-democracy. Therefore, it does not come as a surprise that in his conclusions he returns to themes of democracy in the digital era, and the use of technology as a tool for enlarging the boundaries of traditional democracy. This part of the book provides the most promising substance for future debates. The idea that digital technologies are a powerful weapon in the hands of illiberal states and hostile hackers is gaining ground even among the most enlightened observers. Vilella's suggestion to build 'representative innovation' constitutes a strategic contribution for both political and administrative actors in the Parliament, as well as a concrete work programme for the current Parliament's decisive term.

The European project will need to prepare itself for fresh attacks both internally and externally. It will require a programme that not only defends fundamental principles, but that is also proactive in mobilising the appropriate technologies. Here the author notes, "The defence of democracy cannot be static since an immutable system cannot be defended".

As a Director General at the European Parliament for many years, Vilella is acutely aware of how critically important a collective effort by public administration is in shifting from the comfort zone of 'business as usual' to the stormy world of the digital arena. The challenge lies in explaining issues to an audience that is often hostile to the elite and distrusts 'competence'. European and national bureaucracies cannot avoid these new realities and must leave behind the superior attitudes that are no longer accepted in an age of unrestricted visibility.

A final remark shines a light on the origin of Vilella's case study. The author spent ten months as Research Fellow in the Robert Schuman Centre for Advanced Studies at the European University Institute (EUI), in the framework of an institutional agreement between the EUI and the European Parliament. The fruitful intellectual contribution to the Institute's research profile during his fellowship cements the notion that bridging the gap between academia and the world of practice represents a powerful resource to confront the new challenges of today's European Union. The mutually beneficial relationship between researchers and practitioners promotes informed policymaking to counter the political propaganda that works against the nurturing of European culture. The model of tolerance and understanding that the European Union and the EUI have been shaping since the beginning of their existence will go a long way in fighting those "things you people wouldn't believe".

July 2019

Table of Contents

Scope

This study focuses on the review and adoption of management methods in the European Parliament[1]: the objective is to understand what are the elements that will define the European Parliament Administration (EPA) in the future, from as the 2019 elections to the next years. The Secretary General of the European Parliament, Klaus Welle, addressing his staff after the elections of May 2019 said[2]: "*Now that the citizens have chosen their future, our responsibility will be to accompany and assist their new representatives in the European Parliament in taking up their duties*": indeed, administration capacity is a prerequisite for delivering the institution's mission and objectives. The administration must build on solid foundation the ability to reflect today's needs and anticipate tomorrow needs. To understand which foundations the EPA has chosen is the scope of this study: to do so I will develop the analysis in three parts.

First: No administration can set its managerial approach independent of external forces that affect its activity in a more or less direct way. The administration of a political institution such as the European Parliament must take into account external factors and the environment in which it acts, even more than other administrations. This is why developing the present analysis needs, first of all, to recall the challenges that the European Union is facing nowadays: immigration,

---

[1] The analysis contained in this study is the specific result of a ten-month fellowship at Robert Schuman Centre for Advanced Studies, in European University Institute, Florence. However, my experiences in universities Statale di Milano and Politecnica delle Marche have been of fundamental help.

[2] Internal communication sent on 29 May 2019.

terrorism, nationalism/sovereignism, populism and sometime forms of authoritarianism (illiberal democracy), all undermining the citizens' European feeling. They are all elements that are changing the old political balance (in terms of both political families and inter-States relationships[3]) and fostering the crisis of the European sentiment.

Second: The review and adoption of management methods: the path followed by this study starts with an analysis of the experience garnered in recent years thanks to the introduction of the planning method together with the matrix and metrics approach. It continues by analysing the emergence, in parallel, of technological innovation as a factor in strengthening the development of representative democracy, which the EP administration is in place to serve. But technology is also a supporting factor in the idea of an administrative ecosystem, where people, space and tools are interconnected and inseparable. Then I examine the consequence of all of this on modern management, of which the concept of knowledge sharing is a crucial pillar. Finally, the results of the analysis are taken into account by placing them in the current context and evaluating their possible outlook.

Third: The conclusions highlight how this entire exercise is closely linked to the destiny of democracy. The European Union indeed has democracy among its founding and fundamental values, affording it a central role. The European Parliament is the most direct and strong expression of European democracy, so its administration, the EPA, endeavours to make it work and strengthen it. Precisely because democracy is a European value, the challenges of the contemporary world must be faced head on, first and foremost by fostering the trust of citizens. In the development of modern democracy, administration has an essential role.

---

[3]G. Vilella, *Being European*, Nomos Verlag, Baden Baden, 2017.

In many passages or in whole chapters of this study, I use the pronoun "we" or the adjective "our": this is due to the fact that I have been an integral part of the European parliamentary administration for thirty years. That makes this study not only an analytical contribution but also a personal testimony.

Chapter 1

Facing Challenges

What we have seen in recent years in the crisis of European sentiment includes one fact: it is more and more difficult to analyse the root causes of it[1]. One element evidently emerges in the populist[2] and / or sovereign approach and / or illiberal democracies: the search for a scapegoat for the problems that must be solved. The EU is first on the list of "guilty" parties and is therefore added to the list of enemies to attack. But what, after all, is it that makes such an anti-European approach possible or even attractive?

---

[1]The following reflections are the fruit of an event held at the University of Milan on 22 October 2018: namely the *lectio magistralis* given by the Secretary General of the European University Institute, Vincenzo Grassi on "*The crisis of European sentiment: causes, origins and outlook*", followed by comments made by three eminent professors, M. Florio, A. Martinelli and J. Ziller. On a similar approach, see M. Piantini, *La parabola d'Europa*, Donzelli Editore, Roma, 2019. See also, for a wider point of view, R. Dehousse, *The Euro Crisis and Beyond: The Transformation of the European Political System*, RSCAS 2018/67 Robert Schuman Centre for Advanced Studies, December 2018: the author shows that there has been "a massive transfer of authority to the European level in areas such as macroeconomic policy and banking regulation, which have enormous implications over a large range of public policies ... it has to date aggravated the European democracy conundrum: the Union and its policies are more present in domestic political debates, but they are increasingly contested".

[2]The use here of the term "populist" (or populism) has neither political weight nor is it meant to be denigrating. It is exclusively used in an academic way to support this analysis. Moreover, even the actors defined as "populist" now accept this appellation.

There is, first, a historical-structural factor that is decisive: the context in which the European community was born has completely changed and the political forces that built it have disappeared or are in sharp decline. We must bear in mind that the architects of European unity envisaged, in that context, an ever-growing progressive path but did not think of mechanisms to deal with serious crisis and situations: this fact has been noted over the last ten to fifteen years characterised by situations of serious economic, social and international crisis[3]. Although the answers provided at European level have been substantial, there is no doubt that the difficulties encountered in acting have been and remain enormous because of the lack of intergovernmental solidarity and the lack of will in the process of new transfers of sovereignty. On the other hand, citizens have not reacted by asking their leaders for more supranational decisions because they do not feel like the European construction is a component of their citizenship. In fact, the judgment handed down by citizens about the responses given to crises is not based on an objective analysis of the results and the complex situation, but on their initial expectations, which are independent from the understanding of what actually happens. Reviving pro-European feeling is, under these conditions, extremely difficult, especially as the merits of a united Europe (peace and well-being) have been neglected for at least two generations. There are those who say that a common external enemy could have a unifying force, but there are others who ask what to do even in the absence of an external enemy. In fact, without even looking for an external enemy, I believe that there are already external pressures strong enough to require unity of purpose, while, internally, actions that favour a sense of belonging should be privileged: but the national states and their governments remain the main actors that stand in the way.

These issues are addressed in a recent analysis of Europe history, from the 1950s to the present day[4]: it concludes that the current period of European history is the most peaceful, the most prosperous and freest, the countries of the European Union live in peace, enjoy

---

[3]"L'Europe se fera dans les crises et elle sera la somme des solutions apportées à ces crises", Jean Monnet, *Mémoires*, Fayard, Paris, 1976

[4]I. Kershaw, *Roller coaster: Europe 1950-2017*, Penguin UK, London, 2018.

freedoms and prosperity as never before. Nevertheless, a feeling of insecurity that is greater even than the one felt at the end of the Second World War sweeps the continent[5]. This feeling is a result of numerous factors: not being able to rely on the USA, uncertainty about being able to deal with and resist a new economic crisis, increasing environmental damage, more and more precarious jobs and, as well, atrocities perpetrated by international terrorism. All this taken together is favouring the emergence and establishment of nationalist populism. But, says the analysis, we must keep in mind the fact that this particular political orientation also found fertile ground back in the 1980s, as a result of deindustrialisation and globalisation[6]. They have now been projected forward and strengthened as a result of the migration influxes of 2015 and 2016. In both situations, there was a search (by people) for an ethnic identity to counter international forces and their elites, as well as the newly-arrived migrants: this lead to nationalist populism.

However, this result was not entirely predictable: the weakening of the nation-state could have led to transnationalisation or to a methodological nationalism. Nevertheless, the most evident phenomenon is populist nationalism, the reason for which must also be sought in cultural elements that have created the conditions favourable for its success. Here is a list that derives from an acute analysis.[7] One generally overlooked factor is the "googlisation of culture", where cultural heritage is becoming fragmented, rapid and superficial. Then there is the difficulty of finding one's identity in a state that is welcoming to a vast diversity of cultures, while the supranational identity has not succeeded in establishing itself. Finally, there is also the difficulty

---

[5]Barack Obama, in a landmark speech at the United Nations in 2016, defined this situation as the "paradox" of the contemporary world: we, he said, have never been better off in human history and yet still we feel unhappy.

[6]Recently, a new analysis of the phenomena underway argues that antagonism towards democracy does not derive from the economic crisis but from the search for "dignity" that the market cannot satisfy and which fuels the hatred and aggressiveness expressed on social media: F. Fukuyama, *Identity. The Demand for Dignity and the Politics of Resentment*, Edition Farrar Straus and Giroux, New York, 2018.

[7]Taken from a seminar held at the EUI on 23 January 2019, *Migration, Globalisation and the Nation*, speaker Anna Triandafyllidou.

of recognising oneself in right-wing or left-wing political camps, in a post-1989 world that has progressively liquefied this distinction. As we can see, not only are there socio-political or economic factors, as mentioned above, but also cultural factors that favours the rise of populist nationalism.

To truly grasp what is happening, it helps a great deal to understand the philosophical concept known as "Sleeping Sovereign"[8]. In representative constitutional systems, the government (in the broad sense of institutions as a whole) acts on the basis of the rules established by the sovereign power, i.e. the people, who "remain asleep" except in cases that fall under strict conditions of constitutions or in the event of revolutionary renewal. Among the people, who have the abstract possession of sovereignty, and the government, which holds the concrete and real management of the exercise of power, there is the normative construction that regulates the relationship between the two. To change the normative situation there can be a formal mechanism or there can be a revolutionary mechanism: the latter (in the contemporary world) is not necessarily violent, but can be determined by facts, such as behaviours that impose changes. Now: the EU, as a supra-national authority has the "rationing of sovereignty[9]" approach, which means that it seeks to split the sovereignty of the (no longer) omnicompetent States. The reaction to this condition is the (opposite) approach called "reassertion of sovereignty", which involves the reaffirmation of existing sovereign claims: this determines a new form of sovereigntist consciousness and practice that, articulated in populist terms, reduces pluralism and individual rights. The awakening of the (sleeping) sovereign aims at a drastic renewal of the rules of the game, based on an aspirational project of collective self-rules, to which the populist has an unmediated access. Some have said that

---

[8] As known, it is related to a concept by Thomas Hobbes, to whom the European University Institute dedicated a Max Weber lecture under the title of *"When Sovereigns Stir"*, held by professor N. Walker on 6 December 2018: the reflections that follow are the result of that seminar.

[9] Also this concept, like the previous "sleeping sovereign" and the following "reassertion of sovereignty", originates with Hobbes. It is within this theoretical framework that the approach of F. Fukuyama, *Identity etc. cit.* could find its place.

the current situation is very similar to the prevailing climate in 1919, a phenomenon defined as "nineteenism": at that time one could see a generalised attitude of denying reality and searching for scapegoats, a feeling of widespread fear of losing wellbeing and hostility to the rules of liberal democracy.[10]

Common characteristics of political forces that fall under the populist bracket are to pit the public against the elites, the use of simple political messages and the glorification of the independence of the State[11]. These three characteristics put them on a collision course with the EU, which is seen as being governed by an elite par excellence, which imposes a high degree of competition based on complexity and centralised projects. Even the most sensitive political theory raises important questions[12]: the European Union has presented itself in recent years, in which expectations and crises intersected, as the real testing ground for reconciling democracy and complexity. The EU, as a political space, has the greatest concentration of (political, institutional and administrative) multiplicity and complexity. Hence the fact that European democracy, in the sense of Union, is a complex democracy also from the point of view of political theory. As for European elitism, it is true that at the origins the decision to build what would become the Union has been taken by a ruling elite, which made a courageous decision within a context where it could not have done otherwise. In the meantime, however, society and the concept of democracy have changed, drawing closer to popular sovereignty: the Union has also changed, evolving towards a more democratic system, but not enough compared to external pressures. Therefore, European legitimacy needs more solidity, which is hard to find because Europe was born without the "demos", even if the Treaties then looked for it

---

[10]M. Graziano, in *La Lettura* of 13 January 2019: the author says that this was the breeding ground for fascism.

He also adds that the French "gillets jaunes" are not actually completely poor and are instead the most striking example of this drift.

[11]I pay a debt to the reflections made on 19 October 2018 during the Joint European University Institute/College of Europe Conference, *The Impact of Populism on EU polity and policies* (Fiesole).

[12]For the following remarks see Daniel Innerarity, *La Democracia en Europa*, Galaxia Gutenberg SL, Barcelona, 2017.

and, since Lisbon in particular, they go precisely in that direction.

Today, the EU is more than ever a target worthy of attack because, in this context, it imposes limits on national decisions from a pre-eminent position, requires quality and knowledge in actions and is brought about within a culture of cooperation for multilevel governance[13], characteristics not in keeping with the basic philosophy of populism. An important consequence is that the EU becomes a problematic issue in the national political debate; it is "politicised" as a foreign object. It is not just limited to that either, since Europe is "ideologised". Pro-European sentiment is presented as an ideology and as such must be fought and the European elections are framed as a referendum on who wants Europe and who does not[14].

Added to these common characteristics are the specificities of large regions: in the north-west countries, resistance to the EU is rather on the basis of identity (Islam, immigration, liberalism), in the southern countries it is on socio-economic factors (the economic crisis, slow development) and in the central-eastern countries it is rather on the basis of the defence of nationalism (although they are the great beneficiaries of European economic aid: up to 6/7% of GDP). Then there is the whole aspect of the methods used: the "populist" politician does not accept the check and balance system that they seek to undermine step by step, firstly by always making everything on behalf of the "will of the people" and secondly making controls (which they cannot stand) ineffective through various techniques related to the manipulation of facts and through concessions that are purely cosmetic[15].

---

[13]In the EU, representation exists in multiple and various forms: the EP represents voters, but then there are the national parliaments, the institutions of non-electoral impartiality, the independent institutions, the representation of interests and then there are the national governments. Participatory aspiration must find its own space in this multiplicity but it also clashes with intergovernmental cacophony, which worsens its perception. See Daniel Innerarity, *La Democracia en Europa, etc. cit.*

[14]This acute observation was made by European Parliament Vice-President D.M. Sassoli, at a conference on "*The necessity of correct communication regarding the European elections*", held at the European University Institute on 19 November 2018. D.M. Sassoli has been elected President of the European Parliament in July 2019.

[15]Beyond political institutions, the "populist" wave also begins to attack those

All of this makes it difficult to react from an EU point of view: but this challenge cannot be neglected, we have to take it on and provide answers, not just reactions based on rejection. In order to provide these responses, there is a need for correct communication[16]: but this faces serious obstacles. The biggest is perhaps the lack of information on the mechanisms and functions of the European Union not only at the level of citizens, but also at the level of the media and politicians[17]. This disinformation is certainly fostered by the non-completion of the process of democratic governance, due to an institutional imbalance in favour of national governments, which generates misunderstanding. Another problem arises from the non-concentration of communication (at all levels) on the policies of the European Union, which should instead be at the centre of the debate, as well as the elements that characterise the various actors. The simplicity of the European message to citizens was possible at a time when the single market and many other things still had to be done; they were exciting projects. But once the structures and regulations were put in place and began to work, things got complicated and, in turn, the message did too. In the end, as a consequence of the previous observations, it is up to the ruling classes to promote "awareness" among citizens about the role (also on the global stage) of the Union. One way to address all these difficulties, which will impose itself on the debate in the near future, is the "integration of differences": it is a complicated and delicate issue, with difficult implications not only in the field of law (as

---

independent authorities that have had the most influence and independence when it comes to the management of the drawn-out economic crisis: the central banks. The criticisms and pressures exerted in the last months of 2018 and beginning 2019, both on the governor of the ECB and on the president of the FED are clear signs of this. Independence from politics continues to be championed by these authorities, but the pressure is increasing.

[16]D.M. Sassoli, conference on "*The necessity. . .*" etc. *cit.* Daniel Innerarity, in *La Democracia en Europa*, etc. cit. argues that the EU is not exactly intelligible, although much more than state or regional systems and is therefore difficult to communicate: this does not mean that the process of democratisation is not important or permanent.

[17]D.M. Sassoli, during the conference mentioned above, suggested a sort of "European civic education" in schools. The theme was also addressed in the seminar "*The EP Behind the Scenes: A Discussion with Jean-Paul Denanot*", held at EUI in Fiesole on January 29, 2019.

it is obvious), but also from a philosophical, political, sociological and economic-financial point of view. Yet the reflection has indeed begun.[18]

To summarise, this is what is happening and is directly influencing the activity of the EP administration and which must be taken into account when setting and developing the managerial approach. In crisis management, made difficult by the lack of cooperation between Member States, the EU provides objectively valid and effective responses, but that are far from the expectations that have been created (and have been fuelled) over the last few decades. As a result, the EU is seen as an enemy. Reducing the gap between responses and expectations is a duty of the institutions, the priority over which must be given to the administration. Moreover, the aforementioned EU-enemy sentiment is further fuelled by the perception of the Union as an elite-governed body that issues complex messages and exercises supremacy over the nation-states. These elements are all immediately attributable to the administration's responsibility, which must therefore take account of this pressure when carrying out its activities, including providing information. Furthermore: the increasing intolerance towards the checks and balances of powers and external controls also shine a light on the administration's actions, which are on the front line of guaranteeing the balanced functioning of the system. Finally, as we have seen, all these elements are based on the historical phenomenon of reasserting sovereignty and an awakening of people that increases the demand for legitimation of institutions (in general and) especially European: administration is one of the institutions' pillars of acceptance.

In addition to these elements, which we could define as being more political and cultural in nature, our contextual framework is completed by a new factor of historical significance: namely, the invasive effect of new technologies on our daily lives and the functioning of our modern democracy[19]. The use of technologies, artificial intelligence

---

[18]The European University Institute has launched research under H2020: Integrating Difference in the European Union (InDivEU). The kick-off meeting was held in Fiesole on 24 January 2019.

[19]The EUI organised a workshop focused on an in-depth analysis of this issue on 25 January 2019 entitled *E-Democracy*, with a high-level panel: B. Laffan,

and algorithms in the management of relations with the public in all its aspects, from the economic to the political, is gaining in momentum. As has been very rightly observed, new technologies have immense input on political work and influence policy decisions: the EP accepts the challenge of change that this implies and can and wants to play a central role in future developments, including by encouraging citizen abilities. This process improves over time, because its effective functioning develops tools and methods, while E-Democracy does not transform a citizen into an e-citizen, the citizen remains and must remain a citizen, tout court.[20] In politics this risks filling the void created by the process of disintermediation which, instead of meaning an increase in the democratisation and the empowerment of civil society, becomes facet of manipulation[21]: algorithms and artificial intelligence, in fact, polarise public opinion in a non-transparent manner. The power of technologies can facilitate manipulation and fake news, which is difficult to counter by those who want to establish a political debate based on facts and accuracy. But when it comes down to it, manipulation and lying in politics is a very ancient and well-analysed phenomenon[22]. Nevertheless, untruths told in order to reap political benefits nowadays have the potential to reach a vast audience more effectively and can have devastating effects on democracy.The difficulties that are emerging are new pressures, new demands, new relations with citizens and, on the other hand, the

---

G. Umbach, D.U. Galetta, L. Orgad, T. Karapiperis and Vice-President of the European Parliament Fabio Massimo Castaldo, who played a central role in the discussion. I had the honour of giving the keynote speech.

[20]These are among the many inputs offered by Vice-President F.M. Castaldo during the EUI workshop on *E-democracy cit.*

[21]It is important to bear in mind that during *The Impact of Populism etc. cit.* conference, I gave a presentation on the experience of the European Parliament in making technologies an instrument of a modern democracy and not of the populist approach aimed at eliminating intermediation.

[22]A *Reading group on lying in politics* (enlivened by prof. S. Kröger) was founded at the European University Institute with the intent of examining the various aspects of the problem: H. Arendt,*Truth and Politics*, originally published in The New Yorker, February 25, 1967, was taken as the starting text of the various analyses. Further study on the issue was then continued with the examination of the fundamental texts of Michael Walzer (1973), Sissela Bok (2004), Kant, Rousselière and so on.

continuing undefined issue of the role of the member states.

The European Parliament is fully involved in all the issues mentioned so far and is probably the one actor, more than others, that is best placed to help and find the right solutions. The European Parliament is certainly today the most important and emblematic institution of modern representative democracy[23] and, because of this, it constitutes an essential and unique reference point for the democracy of the future. The reasons are varied, but among the most important we can say that the EP:

- deals with phenomena on the world stage that are at the highest level of complexity
- deals with the most complicated rules on the economy and civil life found at international level
- seeks to find valid solutions for a mixed society with different cultural and legal approaches
- must face up to not one but many governments that pursue national interests
- must take into account a population composed of citizens from many nations who express multiple needs and ideas.

The EP has demonstrated that it knows how to do it and is up to the challenge. An analysis of the activities of the EP in the eighth legislature shows a powerful, original and ambitious, ever-growing EP. A decisive legislator that laid the foundations for 21st century regulations on climate, copyright, protection of data, posted workers, Frontex and trade distortions among just some of the very important examples. The EP has also shown itself to be a solid and respected controller as well as a constant reference point for citizens[24].

All this must be done while respecting the rules of democracy and supporting the further development of democracy, by widening the boundaries of pure representativeness. The EP is in fact at the forefront of protecting rights, ensuring activities are transparent, pro-

---

[23]See, most recently, N. Lupo - A. Manzella, *Il Parlamento europeo. Una introduzione*, Luiss University Press, Roma, 2019.

[24]In this regard, see the great analysis by Ch. Verger (rapporteur), *Le Parlement européen un parlement différent*, Décryptage, 3 May 2019, Notre Europe, Paris.

tecting privacy and encouraging participation.

In pursuing these objectives, the EP has embarked on a path of technological innovation that is essential to keeping up with the times and, at the same time, has launched a review of the management methods that should lead to a way of working more suited to the contemporary world. And, although the EP is a political institution, its actions are based on administrative activities. Efficacy and efficiency are sought by making decisions at the most appropriate level, and by developing appropriate organisation structures and skills at all level in the administration.

The "political" context evolves and in our epoch, historical movements are more rapid than they were in the past: nevertheless, we should expect the phenomena analysed in this chapter to last for some years, although they will change in intensity. Moreover, after the European elections in May 2019, the new composition of the political groups will make policy and future-leaning debates very intense, mixed and strongly dialectical (if not actually confrontational)[25].

Organisations have a constant need to rethink themselves in order to evolve and be in sync with the broader context: the EPA (European Parliament Administration) is certainly a study case that, as we see in the following pages, shows a high degree of excellence in this approach. As we will see in the next chapters, in its recent transformational journey the EPA has always referred to the external context when establishing its strategic objectives.

We must continue to do so: this chapter on "facing challenges" is just a contribution in order to understand what we must take into account when it comes to the future evolution of EP administration and its management. There are certainly many other aspects, but here have been highlighted the main ones:

As regards the context:

- crisis of European sentiment
- feeling of insecurity
- emergence and establishment of nationalist populism

---

[25]On the different possible ways of developing the debate, including the risks of blocking, see M. Telò, *Les élections européennes: le risque de "muddling through"*, in Actualité Carte blanche, IEE, Brussels, 28 May 2019.

- reassertion of sovereignty (*Sleeping Sovereign*)
- incorrect communication # lack of information on the EU mechanisms
- integration of differences
- invasive effect of new technologies

As regards the possible actions:

- Managing crisis
- Being in sync with expectations
- Reducing the perception of being an elite organisation,
- Making an effort in simplifying the message
- Strengthening the cooperation with Member States
- Widening the boundaries of modern democracy by involving citizens.

Chapter 2

Planning, Metrics & Matrix

The starting point for changes in the functioning of the parliamentary administration was the 2009-2011 period during which the new Secretary General, Klaus Welle, introduced a planning method through the establishment of the Administrative Work Program (AWP): it was nothing revolutionary in itself, since it was still up to each Directorate General to draw up a list of projects to be implemented within a given period. But the disruptive element in all this was that the administration of the EP (and it was not the only one in this regard) was not well practiced at all in the planning of projects: this gave rise to uncertainties and sometimes juxtaposition. The main argument against the change put forward was that activities of the EP are not subject to planning, are not translatable into projects or verifiable (in the sense of measurable). But why? In my opinion, it has never been explained why the EP's type of activities are not 'programmable', but more or less it was claimed that dynamic nature and randomness of the activities, due to politics, required operators to constantly adapt and keep pace with current trends. There are no written documents to support this position, but having participated in the discussion itself, I will rely on my experience. In truth, even assuming that this dynamic-random element is present, there was not and there is no reason to think that the EP's activities cannot be adapted to the planning method: on the contrary, I think that their fusion is extremely beneficial. Another argument against the method was that "there is too much work, there is no time to devote oneself to planning", which was obviously an inconsistent argument put forward by those who just wanted a quiet life at work. This is quite a widespread attitude in the world of work, not only in the public sector, and it has been subject to scientific research, even recently: "innovation-killing" observations, essentially of a socio-cultural nature, are produced by an organisation of immovable work that generates conventions and habits[1].

Eventually an AWP was launched and due to both the uncertainties and inexperience it was mostly the sum of micro-projects. The fact that three colours - green, yellow, red - were used to indicate the degree of implementation of the project also aroused fears of being judged, which were understandable but unjustified fears. Just because a project is not carried out on time is not in itself a negative fact. Nevertheless, this fear helped lead to the development of non-ambitious projects: the moral competition was in fact on the collection of "greens" and not on the quality of the project. Things would have changed later, but for the moment the Directors-General were asked to present the results and then present a final report to the President of the EP[2]. This was composed of a volume that collated more than a hundred charts related to the projects of each Directorate-General, where their individual situations were explained by responding to six points:

- targets and deadlines
- status of implementation
- responsible in the DG
- next actions and steps
- decisions required (date/body)
- cooperation with other DGs.

With conviction or not, everyone did their reporting work and in the end there was only one "red" (!), related to the Luxembourg-based

---

[1] See the excellent and in-depth essay by I. Ortenzi, *Innovation manager*, Franco Angeli Editore, Milan, 2018. The author proposes, where possible, the creation of an innovation manager position to guide changes.

[2] *Report to the President. Implementation of the Administrative Work Programme 2009-2011*, Brussels, December 2011.

KAD building project: an outcome not very credible, although "normal" at this early stage.

As I said, this was just the starting point. Already in parallel with the delivery of the Report to the President, the Secretary General introduced another new element aimed at raising the level of planning ambition: it was an analysis of the context in which the EP acts with an outlook looking forward ten years and beyond, contained in the document *The European Parliament 2025 - Preparing for complexity*[3]. This analysis was completed a couple of months later through a study produced by Policy Department D, requested by the EP Bureau: *MEP 2025 - Preparing the Future Work Environment for Members of the European Parliament*[4]. These two documents are of particular importance in the evolution of the EP's management, because for the first time a real outlook based on multidisciplinary analyses was offered up. In the first case *"Preparing"* produced an analysis according to which four elements would influence future developments towards 2025: the new multi-polar context, the multi-level governance, the multi-actors policy making and the technology as a multiplayer in the speed of change. The EU needs to be able to speak with one single voice in the multi-polar context, to rationalise the institutional relations within the multi-level governance, to build and consolidate the networks for managing the multi-actors policy making and to reach a high level of technological capability in its activities. The EP obviously has to follow these global developments, equip itself and adapt. The study concludes with over one hundred questions asked to the EP management, to which it was necessary to give a perspective answer. In the second case, *"MEP 2025"*, the attention is focused on the potential created by information technology and on the changes that it imposes on the functioning of political institutions. The study identifies three areas in which the EP should focus its attention, namely: communication around the democratic process, information management and innovative structure. More specifically, the study then highlights twenty actions to be carried out in these

---

[3]Brussels, January 2012.
[4]Brussels, March 2012 (Vice-president responsible R. Wieland).

three areas, which I will return to in the following chapter (Technology).

These two studies and in-depth reflections had a very important impact on the planning method. The "*Preparing*" document ended as we saw with a (long) series of questions, which were submitted to the management of all the directorates-general, with a request to provide answers from their point of view, not only limited to their field of competence. The result is an original document that presents the answers provided, in a collective exercise never carried out before[5]. It is a method that in some way left its mark and above all offered a picture of how the EP management sees its work and imagines it in the long-term perspective: although there have been no immediate practical effects, this is an important element in the evolution of the administration of the European Parliament. In the summary that the Secretary General drew from it[6], the elements needed to cope with these rapid changes in the evolution of the EP are highlighted: the EP has to become a learning organisation that has permanent updating in its structures, procedures, staffing, training and equipment. To do this correctly we need a strategic approach that looks at long-term problems. For each aspect considered there are organisational consequences, like the creation of a unit specialised in the scrutiny economy, more contacts with national experts, a new role for the information offices, closer collaboration with the Committee of the Regions and the Economic and Social Committee, greater support for MEPs in their constituencies and many other solutions that were then implemented over time. The report concludes by raising the question as to whether the EP should also think about involving citizens in the legislative process via new technologies.

At the same time, the EP Bureau launched a parallel initiative[7], which assumes central importance in the improvement of parliamentary management: this involves the revision, for the purpose of clarification and simplification, of all the internal rules and procedures of

---

[5]CSG EP 2025 Team, *Preparing for complexity*, Brussels March, 2013 (Responsible for EP 2025 process: F. Debié).

[6]K. Welle, *Preparing for complexity - Final Report*, April 2013.

[7]Based on a report prepared by Vice-president D. Roth-Behrendt.

the EP[8], which often suffer from a problem of hierarchy of sources, of inconsistency or of overlapping, not to mention the panoply of notes, codes and communications that create a soft law that is not obligatory and therefore sometimes confusing. It was revealed that some rules are inaccessible or even do not have an exact date attached or are not properly sourced. The recommendations made by the task force were and remain extremely valid and should be implemented with rigour:

- Establishment of a general procedure to be followed for any new rule
- Unification of terminology, in order to express the same concepts in different rules
- Systematic publication of newly adopted internal rules
- Presentation of the new rules
- Publication of rules as a prerequisite for their entry into force
- Recasting and consolidation, in order to avoid an incomprehensible pile-up of reforms
- Creating a specific publication of currently applicable rules.

Transparency, clarity and easy access to rules are essential elements needed for good management. The clarity and simplicity of the rules applicable within an organisation is a fundamental factor to foster correct management: although the result of this work was truly exceptional in analysing the situation, unfortunately the initiative did not have a tangible or significant follow-up.

As demonstrated, the years 2011-2013 saw a strong maturation in the evolution of the EP management: firstly, with the introduction of context and perspective analysis, which elevated ambitions, and secondly through the importance attached to administrative simplification. All this exerted great influence on the exercise of the AWP and at the same time prepared the ground for a new leap in quality with the new legislature. As for the AWP itself, the method of presentation and evaluation was changed at that point, abandoning the approach of the first Report to the President (2011). In January 2014, a part was added in which projects would have a "corporate" character, i.e. they

---

[8] *Stock-taking of the internal rules and administrative procedures applied in the European Parliament: conclusions of the Administrative Task Force on Simplification*, Brussels 16 December 2013 (Vice-president responsible D. Roth-Behrendt).

are aimed at a common goal, which in this case is the strengthening the European Parliament: in this part each project had a framework with a description and objectives and another framework entitled "current state of play of implementation", where a long explanatory narrative was developed. It therefore morphed from a purely schematic plan to the analytical-explanatory plan of the project. Moreover, these "corporate" projects were framed within broader themes, which allowed them to escape the limbo of isolated initiatives: these projects were now part of a broader strategic objective (which actually numbered ten) destined to strengthen the EP as a whole. The rest of the AWP remained focused on the projects of the individual DGs, but the presentation was very different from the archaic one used until 2011: in the new report there is space for the description and the objectives, another includes the background, then there is a detailed description of the planning and a framework that contains additional explanatory comments (these remain the recommendations of the responsible DG, but it is now becoming something nominative, and a matter of internal cooperation)[9].

This is the final stage of the first phase of the new planning approach (2009-2014) and it, together with the analysis of the future outlook and the legislation, prepares the ground for the qualitative leap offered by the new legislature thanks to the introduction of the SEF-PPP where the SEF (Strategic Execution Framework) is the method and the PPP (Parliament Project Portfolio) is the tool. Even this new approach required a period of maturation, but the leap in quality regarding the AWP has been immediate: obviously there was again not a lack of confusion and criticisms, based essentially on the observation that we were introducing a level of excessive sophistication, unnecessarily high compared to the real needs of parliamentary work. This point deserves attention, but unfortunately the debate was poisoned by the controversy, indeed from the conflict, stemming from another parallel aspect, that of the NWOW (New Way - or World - of Working), which I will return to in a moment.

First we need to understand what the SEF-PPP consists of. The

---

[9]*Administrative Work Programme. January 2014 update* (without further information).

first working document inspired by the new approach dates back to October 2014[10]: all the projects (totalling 127), independent of their responsible directorates general, are classified in nine thematic areas:

- completing the legislative cycle
- improved service to Members in their legislative and political functions
- buildings and logistics programme
- service improvement for Members
- digitalisation of processes
- resource efficient multilingualism
- efficient financial management
- knowledge management
- new world of work.

Each project is presented with an identical explanatory structure which includes, after the title, the following chapters:

- scope/description of the project
- expected outcomes: savings, efficiency gains or service improvements
- responsibility: project sponsor and project manager
- major project milestones and timing.

Once again we should note that this is an evolution of the managerial approach that involves adopting a planning method for projects within a strategic framework for objectives. The PPP, of which the October 2014 working document is the first example, collects the totality of these elements and puts them together. Of course it would be interesting to examine the individual projects (which are numerous) in order to evaluate the merit of the action, but it is not the objective of our analysis. Instead, it is essential to understand how the theoretical basis of support for this method has been conceived, i.e. the SEF.

---

[10]The Secretary General, *Parliamentary Project Portfolio within the Strategic Execution Framework of the European Parliament*, Brussels, October 2014. The main reference in this approach, in the first stage, has been M. Morgan, R.E. Levitt, W. Malek, *Executing your strategy*, Boston, Harvard Business School Press, 2007.

The Strategic Execution Framework, as the first word clearly indicates, places at the centre of its system the strategy around which five large inter-related sets rotate and are made cohesive precisely by the gravitational centre offered by the Strategy. The first set, called Ideation includes Purpose, Identity and Long-range intention, the second, entitled Nature, contains Culture and Structure, while the third, called Vision, includes Goal and Metrics. The other two are called Synthesis and Transition, which contain the Portfolio, the Program, the Project and Operations. All of this is influenced by the external environment, but manages to metabolise the factors and transform them into responses. This is purely an intelligent rationalisation of planning that takes on value when you "fill" the boxes, which we will see in a moment.

Where do the big objectives defined in the SEF-PPP come from? They are the result of reflections on the merits of the issues developed in parallel with the evolution of managerial management. I have already mentioned *Preparing for Complexity* and *MEP 2025*, both dating back to 2012. Then, in April 2014, an important report by the Secretary General[11] took stock of the potential impacts, obligations and responsibilities deriving from the Lisbon Treaty on the EP. The report tries to understand, using the basis of the achievements made in the various sectors during the first years of application of the Lisbon Treaty, what scope there was to expand the role of the EP and, consequently, how the administration should adapt. The analysis is developed along four large sensitive areas (budgetary powers, control over international agreements, new partnerships and appointment-control of the European executive) without wanting to be exhaustive[12], but drawing reflections from these examples. Just a few months after the exercise, it was expanded by focusing on community policies: in the

---

[11]K. Welle (editor), *One Hundred Steps Forward: The European Parliament and the Upgrading of European Democracy since the Lisbon Treaty*, Brussels, April 2014.

[12]A comprehensive picture is provided in *Fact Sheets*: created for Parliament's first direct elections, the Fact Sheets are designated to provide non-specialists with simple, concise and accurate overview of the EU institutions and policies, and the role that the EP plays in their development: last edition published in paper available is of 2017, while the online version is regularly updated.

report, *Rolling legislative agenda of the European Union*[13] looks into the level of political responsiveness of the EP in the fields taken into consideration by the European Council programme *Strategic Agenda for the Union in Times of Changes*[14]. For each sector, the EP document investigates requests made by the Assembly to the Commission and the Council to make legislative initiatives a reality. For each sector, the first analysis was of what has actually been achieved, then what requests from the EP have received a full or partial response and then finally which requests have not been answered or have not yet been made by the EP. Everything was accompanied by coloured explanatory charts to create an immediate visual impact. Another significant example that goes in the same direction is the study into the costs of non-Europe[15] where all the advantages and benefits produced by European Union intervention are identified, particularly, although not limited to, the economy. The current study shows how the EP manages its activities, so it was essential to have pointed out that there is no lack of political analyses supporting the management choices.

It is on this theoretical basis, consolidated by reflection on the political-legislative context and by a logical and continuous evolution of the exercise, that we were able to arrive at the moment of maturity, the Away Day of January 13, 2017 in Aachen where the Secretary General developed the concrete contents of the SEF for the period 2017-2019, i.e. the second half of the 8th parliamentary term[16]. After confirming the constitutive elements of the SEF (of which I have already spoken above) the SG report goes on to fill in the various components with content, starting from the external con-

---

[13]Brussels, September 2014, prepared by the director-generals for internal policies, R. Ribera d'Alcalà,and external policies, M. Aguiriano Nalda, together with the Secretary-General.

[14]Statement by the European Council at the meeting on 27 June 2014.

[15]J. Dunne, *Mapping the Cost of Non-Europe 2014-2019*, Brussels, April 2015, preceded by two versions that have now been updated.

[16]The Secretary General, *Strategic Execution Framework 2017-2019 for the Administration of the European Parliament*, 13 January 2017 (Away Day Final): the seminar was characterised by the presentation of various sectorial reports by management exponents. On that occasion the amusing but effective approach of the Administrative Train, of great visual impact, was also adopted.

text, where it identifies the elements of pressure[17] and the responses that are emerging[18]. It is important to note how each component of the SEF has been "filled in" (defined in practice), because this offers a clear idea of how the SEF is conceived as a working tool in the management of the EP. For what is called Ideation, the SG suggests in his report:

a) for Purpose, that the administration empowers the MEP for a resilient and effective European democracy:

b) for Identity, that the staff is a multinational team building continental democracy for a closer EU;

c) for Long-range intention, that the administration wants to improve services to MEPs through continuous innovation. The services in question concern technical, collective and individual infrastructures, the management of political processes, communication, knowledge support and linguistic services.

For Nature and Vision, the Goals and the Metrics are grouped into six chapters that form the core of the Strategy: Enhanced services, Managing Efficiently, Innovative Working, Completing the Legislative Cycle, Linking the Levels and Succeeding 2019. Each of these chapters in turn is composed of numerous projects attributed to the individual DGs.

For Culture and Structure, there is firstly a shift from a rule-based administration to an administration focused on results, innovation and customer satisfaction. Then it is a case of separate administration in silos transitioning to an administration that works in a Matrix, in continuous cooperation and exchange among the various DGs. The best example of this idea is the Policy Management Team, composed of the SG and all the general managers (which meets at least once a month), while numerous inter-DG committees are organised according to various sectors of activity[19] with the task of jointly monitoring

---

[17] Aggressive Russia, Destabilised Islamic World, Inward focused USA, Brexit, Aftershock of financial crisis, Insecurity by globalisation and technological disruption, Social nationalism on the rise, Challenges by multi-crisis.

[18] Strengthening reform capacity, The Bratislava Agenda, Internal Security, External Security, Social security and growth, Complementary executive capacity, Linking the levels of EU governance.

[19] The Inter-DG Steering Groups are in the fields of: economic policies, struc-

and guiding those activities that remain the responsibility of the responsible administrations.

The PPP (within Synthesis and Transition) is responsible for making the whole approach operational through the projects, which are subdivided into programmes. A sort of coming of age of the new approach was illustrated by the Innovation Day on 12 January 2018, when a 628-page document was presented containing all the projects in progress[20] and some director-generals analysed every strategic programme.

The same scheme was used a year later, during a new Innovation Day. The event was dedicated to one focal theme, *Empowering the Union for the Multipolar World*, and developed along four axes that in turn contain specific insights: the "challenges" of a multipolar world, the citizens "expectations", the overcoming "limitations" and the building of the "executive capacity".[21] The event took place in Brussels all day on 11 January 2019. Despite some perplexities advanced as first impact to the programme, it must be said that the four axes of analysis have a foundation and logic. Let us first look at the perplexities: they derive from the difficult connection between the programme of the event and the administration's innovation, particularly because of the numerous varying and specific themes addressed and the kilometric (and therefore concerning) lists of possible projects they generate. The programme appears to be designed around the sectors rather than looking at the innovation of the EPA. However, beyond the chosen themes and the latter complications, it was very important to bring together a few hundred people with operational responsibilities and put them all together for a whole day, prompting them to exchange ideas and even opinions, whatever they may have been.

---

tural policies, citizens' policies, budgetary policies, external policies, human resources, finance, information technology and, in addition, there is also a Resource Directors Team.

[20]K. Welle (editor), *Strategic Execution Framework for the Administration of the European Parliament 2017-2019*, Brussels, December 2017 (Responsible staff: F. Debié, A. Cabanelas, F. Renuit, S. Rogowski).

[21]European Parliament Administration Innovation Day, 11 January 2019, Agenda.

However, as I said, the four axes have a foundation: it is true that the concept of a multipolar world is not new and is overused, but it is also true that overcoming limitations, citizens' expectations and executive capacity are the real current problems, which the European Union must respond to with clarity and decisiveness, as well as providing answers. The choice of themes responds to the declared will to focus the reflection on political aspects because, as we have seen above[22], the political background is necessary for the proper management development of the EP administration (but, also of all the other institutions). The theme that emerged as the most central, also in the conclusions of the Secretary General, was that of the "expectations gap", in which there is an urgent need to intervene in order to reduce the gap to citizens. Surveys and statistics can certainly help to orient oneself to understand where the malaise comes from, but they (often based on poorly formulated questions) cannot penetrate the profound reasons for the movement taking place in society.

It follows that the administration of the European institutions, primarily the EPA, must take it into account in its action and in its organisation. The question is how to integrate them into administrative planning without complicating it and weighing it down. During the Innovation Day, two supporting publications were distributed. The first is an updated edition of the *Strategic Execution Framework*[23], without structural changes, but with new information on the development of ongoing projects. The second, the *Ideas Papers for the Innovation Day 2019*[24], are a set of introductory reports to the topics dealt with in the event: each report contains an analytical part and a list of projects deriving from it. They (the new projects) number a few hundred, which are in addition to the hundreds contained in the SEF / PPP and in the IT plan (that is adopted by a separate procedure). This is a trend that will be difficult to govern. Despite these difficulties, the Secretary General had in mind a clear process as follow-up of the event: first elaboration of the SEF by each DG[25] fo-

---

[22] See the first chapter on *Facing Challenges.*

[23] Brussels, European Parliament, December 2018 (Responsible: F. Debié)

[24] Twelve ideas papers produced by the European Parliamentary Research Service (s.d., s.l., however Brussels December 2018))

[25] See the draft-document *Strategic Execution Framework 2019-2021.*

cused on "game changer projects" and then assembling the results in a global SEF/PPP in the perspective of the 2019-2024 legislation term. During a meeting at the European Parliament Management Away Days[26] the Secretary-General made a clear reference to the content of the Aachen seminar. In this way, he highlighted the continuity of action over time. Then he emphasised that in the next SEF/PPP there will be a group of ten goals that will be valid for the whole administration, goals that constitute the unifying and corporate moment of the programmatic action. The goals are defined as "determining factors" of the strategy. Finally, the Secretary-General focused in on the "metrics" method, measuring performance, whose importance is fundamental. Little space has been afforded to the Matrix, which should instead be a principle, inspiring element: this aspect has been fully recovered, by making a balance between metrics and matrix, during the Third Management Innovation Day on 30 April 2019. During this event the philosophy of the fourth period has been clearly strengthened and defined[27].

To summarise, we can outline the following steps in the last ten years: First period 2009-2011 // Second period 2012-2014:

- Introduction of the Administrative Work Program (AWP) with final report to the President of the EP
- analysis of the context in which the EP acts
- revision, for the purpose of clarification and simplification, of all the internal rules and procedures of the EP
- a section in which there are "corporate" projects

Third period 2014-2017:

- Introduction of the SEF-PPP where:
    - the SEF (Strategic Execution Framework) is the method

Directorates-General (s.d, s.l., however it is Brussels March 2019).

[26]Held at the Jean Monnet Academy, Bazoches-sur-Guyonne (France) on 14 and 15 March 2019.

[27]As documentation support of the meeting has been distributed: *3rd Management Innovation Day. Contributions of the Directorates-General to the SEF 2019-2021* (K. Welle editor), Brussels, April, 2019; *Europe's two trillion euro dividend. Mapping the Cost of Non-Europe, 2019-24* (A. Teasdale editor), Brussels, April 2019; *Strategic Execution Framework 2019-2021* etc. cit.; and a first version of the present Study.

> − and the PPP (Parliament Project Portfolio) is the tool

- the SEF (Strategic Execution Framework) places at the gravitational centre of its system the strategy around which five large inter-related sets: Ideation, Nature, Vision, Synthesis and Transition, Operations
- after two and half year of experience at Away Day of January 13, 2017 in Aachen: the Secretary General developed the concrete contents of the SEF, defined in practice each of these sets.

Forth period 2017-2019 *preparing the next Legislation term:*

- Innovation day events *:* involving a large part of the staff
- DGs SEF: based on game-changer projects
- SEF/PPP: ten corporate goals and development of metrics.

Chapter 3

Technology, Administration and E-Democracy

In the previous pages, it is made clear that a decisive aspect in defining new working methods in the EP, as elsewhere, is the breakthrough of new technologies in the contemporary world. Their impact on politics, in general, and on the functioning of democracy, more specifically, is significant and is causing profound changes, sometimes even radical ones[1]. The EP saw the importance of the phenomenon relatively early on: in fact the Directorate-General ITEC (Innovation and Technological Support) for support and technological innovation was created in 2007 and was provided with substantial resources that have been increased over time. Moreover, in the two studies already widely cited, *Preparing etc.* and *MEP 2025 etc.* the issue was looked into profoundly in 2012. In the first study (*Preparing*), technologies were labelled as an accelerator that shrinks time and space, creating faster connection, favouring remote localisation and remote activation, imposing a focus on new information management. In the second study (*MEP 2025*), they were described as a factor that contributes to changing the way things work and making society and democracy more horizontal: as consequence the EP was invited to experiment in

---

[1] G. Vilella, E-*Democracy*, Nomos Verlag, Baden-Baden, 2019. The reflections that follow come from the analysis contained in the book, but also from the EUI Workshop on *E-Democracy* etc. cit.

three key areas such communication around the democratic process[2], information management[3], ICT platform or community[4]. Over the course of the following years, all the indications contained in the two documents inspired the internal policies of technological innovation.

DG ITEC was the first to adopt the planning method for managerial choice and immediately adhered to the new EPA approach. The DG was helped along by the fact that the nature of its activities lend themselves to and indeed require planning mainly because of their innovative role and support of other projects. The introduction of an IT Plan, however, was not easy: in the previous phase there had been an irrational accumulation of requests for interventions and ideas for innovation. The problem was not the content of the projects but the total disorder in which they accumulated due to the lack of planning. To overcome this problem, there was a need:

a) to understand ITEC's fulfilment and delivery project capacity;

b) to establish priorities in projects resulting from external requests on the basis of the plans of the individual DGs;

c) to set priorities in corporate projects on the basis of a clear institutional strategy.

The turning point was 2011 like - not surprisingly - the evolution of the AWP. In order to resolve the first aspect of the problem sub a) a detailed analysis was made of the organisational structure and the organisation chart of ITEC, as well as of its working methods. The most serious issues were the confusion of competences between infrastructures and development activities, the division into silos of the units and the lack of cooperation, excessive dependence on external experts and lack of a common vision. All this was remedied (largely, not totally) through important organisational reforms with the indispensable support of the Secretary General. To resolve the second part of the problem sub b), there was a need for a real conceptual and methodological revolution through the introduction of a procedure for adopting the IT Plan. DG ITEC would no longer establish

---

[2]Virtual meetings, e-Consultation, be mobile, use of portable device, websites, cyber security, transparency, multilingualism.

[3]Visualisation techniques, cloud, online archives.

[4]Infrastructural backbone, online collaboration, working from anywhere.

its work plan unilaterally but only after a phase of close consultation with the other DGs, during which each project is then evaluated from two points of view, a timescale is assigned and classified according to priority. I must say that at the end of 2011, a fundamental step was the agreement of all the DGs not to propose new projects for a year to allow ITEC to address the backlog. Since then the IT Plan has been adopted in close collaboration with the DGs and its implementation is assessed both bilaterally and collectively. On this basis it was also possible to introduce forecasts of projects implemented in a decentralised way by the DGs. In order to find a solution to the third problem sub c), all innovation activity in corporate projects must now make a clear reference to the orientations of the political summit, the Bureau, and to the administrative planning flowing into the SEF-PPP analysed in the previous chapter: however, each corporate project must be part of the PPP strategies.

These changes of method have yielded excellent results both in raising the level of delivery and in increasing the quality of support, and in making the management of resources more efficient. But the most important results, which can be defined as exceptional compared to international standards, have been recorded within the framework of instruments that allow Parliament to function in an advanced way, both politically and administratively (which are interdependent):

- Innovative working tools: eCommittee, eMeeting, AT4AM, digital signature, drafting support tool, use of tablets, knowledge management, mobile intranet and directory, unified communication
- Innovative working methods: collaborative workplaces, eParliament 2019, paperless parliament, remote access, teleworking, ICT services in constituencies
- Document production and printing strategy: multilingual data, XML metadata and indexing, multimedia products, cross-media printing
- Internal communication: Intranet and multimedia creation
- ICT security and facilities management: governance, CERT, Data Centre, encryption, monitoring, standard configuration.

This list corresponds, more or less, to the index of a guide produced and disseminated to inform users about the tools available, and where each sector is examined in detail[5]: the listed new tools and methods of work are essential for the development of the analysis, they are in fact the foundation blocks and the constituent elements of modern democracy (or E-Democracy).

The concept of "E-Democracy" is evolving in a contradictory manner[6]: there are those who argue that digital democracy is replacing democracy as we know it today, especially representative democracy and, therefore, the same Parliament that would then be destined to disappear. Evidently this statement has no concrete basis and is not at all plausible, but because of the very fact that it has gained traction, it has become a weapon of pressure and influence at political level, in general, and on parliamentarians much more specifically.

E-Democracy must, on the contrary, be seen as an evolution of representative democracy in the sense of the expansion of its borders and, therefore, in the sense of its strengthening. From society, from citizens, there is a growing demand for connectivity and participation. In this context, technology is changing the way MEPs communicate with citizens, creating a permanent connection that enables not only greater communication, but also greater participation in the democratic process. Technology also allows local MEP's offices, in the constituency, to be included in the EP network, increasing mobility and flexibility: wherever you are, you will be able to access and exchange information with citizens and colleagues, for better, faster and efficient decision-making processes. The capability for MEP to cover multiple channels of communication and to reinforce the bridges between the Parliament and the constituencies will become even more of

---

[5] *Innovative Working in the European Parliament. A guide*, Brussels, November 2016. The guide also contains a USB stick with various videos explaining the individual products. On this subject, there was an analytical reflection during the Policy Dialogue European Parliament/European University Institute on "*European Parliament Elections - Challenges and Opportunities of new Digital Technologies*" held on 18 ottobre 2018. The meeting was chaired by M. Tell Cremades, I gave a presentation on the solutions prepared by the EP.

[6] In my book G. Vilella, *E-Democracy*, etc. cit., I make a thorough and detailed analysis of this topic, together with an extensive bibliography that I will limit only to a mention here.

an asset in the democratic role of the European Parliament[7].

It must be clear that very rapid technological developments have an immediate and strong impact on the democratic system: politics, legislator and case-law are forced to deal with this on a daily basis, going down new and unknown paths. Technological innovation is changing, or rather has changed the relationship between representatives and the people they represent, between the people elected and the people who elect them, and it is now starting to influence the party system as well. It is seen by some as an instrument of direct democracy, and by others as a driving force which is a danger to democracy. There is also the decrease of privacy, internet users' profiles being exploited at will and users being steered to specific sites for commercial gain. All these issues go hand in hand with the problems regarding the controversial right to be forgotten and the intellectual property, with illegal downloads and many other issues. There is also indiscriminate monitoring by "big brother" of our freedom of communication, now faltering under increasingly frequent and complex cyber attacks.

There is a multiplying factor to problematic aspects: culturally, the current tendency is to be constantly online, to the point of being internet dependent, which can become a genuine health disorder. We have now reached the paradoxical situation of having to use machines to free ourselves of them. Some people believe that this phenomenon is changing our way of thinking and reflecting. Others, however, believe that modern technology is improving teaching and learning techniques and opening the door to new possibilities and renewed creativity.

Lastly, there is the fact that technological innovation is now pivotal for the economy and growth. ICT is changing the way that companies structure themselves and operate – not just in the macroeconomy, but in the microeconomy as well. ICT companies are listed on stock exchanges more than any others in the world. However, ICT

---

[7]The Vice-president E. Gebhardt, in charge (2017-19) of ICT and Cybersecurity, has written (*Foreword to Technological Innovation and democracy*, Brussels, May 2017):"There is no doubt that our democracies rely on the capacity to create a trusting relationship between elected representatives and their constituencies ... an everyday challenge in which technology plays a key role, contributing to strengthen the EP as a representative of the citizens of European Union".

also influences the labour market, not just by creating new professions and jobs[8], but also by helping to match up supply and demand and making the market more dynamic.

So, looking at its impact on law, culture, economy and the politics[9], it is easy to see that technological innovation underpins a huge well of power in today's world. Every innovation in political and administrative matters is now totally dependent on technology: it must understand the political context in which it is operating if the end result is to be efficient and effective. Administration and politics are thoroughly integrated into technology, and vice versa.

A big problem, in my opinion, is the fact that today, there are general conditions brought about by the rapid and widespread development of technological innovation, which produce and foster powers which it is difficult to curb or control, and which are concentrated: something that will presumably increase in the near and far-off future, exacerbating the problem. Montesquieu, who defended the separation of powers and opposed absolute powers, was unfamiliar with such a situation and indeed could never have imagined or anticipated it, and yet nowadays law and theory are endeavouring to manage this phenomenon like any other issue to be regulated and incorporated into the traditional system. It is not – or rather, it is not only that: in

---

[8]On this specific (and sensitive) issue, the EUI organised an important Roundtable on *World Bank 2019 World Development Report "The Changing Nature of Work"*, 4th of April 2019 in Florence: Fears that robots will take jobs have dominated the discussion on the future of work, but the Report finds that on balance this appears to be unsubstantiated. Work is constantly reshaped by technological progress. Firms adopt new ways of production, markets expand, and societies evolve. Overall, technology brings opportunity, creating new jobs, increasing productivity, and delivering effective public services. I participated in the panel as discussant.

[9]Of not secondary importance, in the world of politics, is the impact that new technologies are having on diplomatic activity. The EUI organised a major Cyber Dialogue event on the topic of Supporting EU Cyber Diplomacy and, in this context, a roundtable entitled: *"Towards a Cyber Union? The EU's added value in managing complexity in cyberspace"*, which was held in Fiesole on 28 January 2019. The aim is to promote the Cyber Dialogue between the EU and other global partners, on the basis of international law but also of soft law, confidence measures and state resilience: in fact, it is very clear that the competence of the sector remains at national level (in response to my explicit question).

sober fact, it is a phenomenon which produces "power" in the full meaning of the term, a separate power, which is wielded with frightening force in the presence of other, traditional, powers. Only a solid link between the political level and the administration level can face the problem with possibilities of success: that is why the task of the European Parliament administration is at the very least important, if not essential.

However, technology is not only a source of worrying problems for the political system: there is a wealth of factors which, thanks to technological innovation, help to make governmental authority stronger and more effective[10]. Firstly, it is an excellent tool for making public action more transparent and promoting public participation[11]. It is also an excellent tool for reinforcing the work of parliament or any other political level along with the administration. According to the European Parliament Resolution of 16 March 2017[12], "democracy should evolve and adapt to changes and opportunities related to new ICT technologies and tools", a statement that expresses the clear awareness of a process of change in progress. According to the Resolution we are in an age of increasing disaffection on the part of citizens towards politics, so there is a clear need to improve the democratic

---

[10]The international conference *Law via Internet - Knowledge of the Law in the Big Data Age* (Florence, 11-12 October 2018) went even deeper into these issues: Sandro Mameli and I presented the case of the European Parliament, with a particular focus on the legislative process.

[11]This topic was the subject of a seminar held by the European University Institute: *Legislative Transparency in the European Union: What can happen after recent Luxembourg Jurisprudence* (Fiesole, 16 October 2018, rapporteur E. De Capitani): it has been pointed out that transparency as a pillar of modern democracy cannot be treated with a bureaucratic approach, and that in order for it to be effective in citizen participation it cannot only be completed at the end of the process.

[12]P8_TA(2017)095. The European Parliament's Resolution concludes with an explicit reference to an Italian initiative. In the penultimate paragraph it says that the European Parliament "calls on the European institutions to launch a participatory process in order to elaborate a European Charter of Internet Rights, taking as reference, among other texts, the Declaration of Internet Rights published by Italy's Chamber of Deputies on 28 July 2015, in order to promote and guarantee all the rights pertaining to the digital sphere, among them the genuine right of access to the internet and net neutrality".

link between institutions and citizens, who need to express themselves more frequently and more directly: citizen involvement is now judged to be essential to the functioning of democracy. To cope with this situation, the European Parliament considers "that digital democracy tools can help promote more active citizenship, improving participation, transparency and accountability in decision-making, strengthening control mechanisms and knowledge".

To sum up on technology as support of the concept of «e-Democracy»:

- there are those who argue that digital democracy is replacing representative democracy and, therefore, that the same Parliament is destined to disappear
- E-Democracy must, on the contrary, be seen as an evolution of representative democracy in the sense of the expansion of its borders and, therefore, in the sense of its strengthening
- from society, from citizens, there is a growing demand for connectivity and participation

Technology is

- changing the way MEPs communicate with citizens,
- creating a permanent connection that enables greater information sharing,
- allowing greater participation in the democratic process
- allowing local MEP's offices, in the constituency, to increase mobility and flexibility
- an excellent tool for making public action more transparent and promoting public participation
- an excellent tool for reinforcing the work of parliament or any other political body.

It means that administration must adapt to the new reality. In fact, what has academia[13] been asked about the attitude of the ad-

---

[13]I refer specifically to an event called: *Stato e Amministrazione di fronte alla rivoluzione delle ICT: partecipazione, diritti e nuovi attori*, which was held in Milan on 7 May 2019. Organised by the International and European Public Law Doctorate and the Department of Social and Political Sciences (organisational secretary Dr Paolo Provenzano), was chaired and coordinated by prof. Diana-Urania Galetta with prof. Gabriele Bottino, prof. Tommaso Edoardo Frosini and

ministration (and political institutions) to the ICT revolution? A revolution, it certainly is, but it is a revolution "in progress" and not one of those rapid and destructive upheavals. The revolution is here, it is underway but it is developing step by step, perhaps with a fast march but still one step after another. To be clear and precise, no one has been wiped out by his role, be it as a lawyer, university professor, politician or, as far as we are concerned, an administrative officer: we are all here to try to adapt to this innovative evolution, to the ongoing revolution. This statement here is far from being just a secondary one. In fact, how do you deal with ICT-induced changes? You can be taken by surprise by the phenomenon and, once you have verified its existence, you can be "reactive" and respond to pressures caused by the revolution. The previous statement (a revolution, yes, but in progress) helps us find the right answer: more than a "surprise" though we have to talk about a "delay" in understanding the phenomenon: is this subtlety important? Extremely, because if you are caught by surprise you are lost, while you can recover from a delay: this is true in legal regulation, at work, in political action and, for what concerns us, in administrative action. The EPA actually already works to govern change.

To conclude, when speaking of "e-Democracy", we must bear in mind both sides of the coin, which illustrate the complexity of an evolving phenomenon. We are still taking our first steps, and the result of this mix of dark and positive aspects[14] of the power of technology is not yet clear. Because it is intimately connected to the various aspects of daily life, because it plays a key role in the development of human activity and has an impact on people's daily lives, we know and understand reality through the lens of technological innovation and its unstoppable progress. And because we see reality through the development of technology, we can extend this realisation to the fact that in our daily role as public managers, we need to

---

lawyer Carmelo Fontana, with the conclusions entrusted to me.

[14]Vice-President F.M. Castaldo rightly pointed out during the aforementioned workshop on *E-Democracy* that we must be very careful when making lists of positive things and negative things caused by the use of technology in politics. What are the criteria that are used to define the positive and the negative, and from which point of view (and whose) a certain effect is positive or negative?

have a better understanding of just how the world around us is changing through technology in order to understand, and steer, the digital
transformation of our EP administration, including the workplace.

Chapter 4

Administrative Ecosystem

Technology is also a constituent element of the concept of administrative ecosystem. The concept of "administrative ecosystem[1]" or the EP as an ecosystem was introduced for the first time during the Administration Away Days in Aachen, January 2017: the idea is that people, spaces and tools interact constantly and cannot be considered separately when organising activities and managing resources, because the ecosystem approach amplifies the potential of all its elements[2]. In fact, all the technological tools mentioned in the previous chapter create the conditions necessary for this to happen, for the simple reason that the support provided by parliamentary administration to the political action is no longer the same as it has traditionally been and it can no longer go in search of efficiency in the classical way. In a highly digitalised European Parliament, our workplace is now more mobile and more flexible, enabling very high level of interaction and more efficient use of data: we are constantly in touch with political

---

[1]The term "ecosystem" may actually lead to misunderstandings, because it is originally a term used in biological sciences. However, now the term has also been borrowed by social sciences and management studies to indicate the interconnections existing between various sectors, necessary for global equilibrium.

[2]One study that clearly shows how the "ecosystem" approach to management produces efficiency and enhances the use of available resources is F. Caselli, *Technology differences over space and time*, Princeton University Press, Oxford, 2017: the book shows how coordinating the use of workers, skills, equipment and structures makes the countries that do so richer and more advanced.

and practical information, readily available and transferable to the widest number of people. We can expect an increase in the pace of innovation, and that our way of working will become more-and-more mobile and flexible: further, it will certainly require an adaptation of working space and working time based on an anywhere/anytime approach.

Serious reflection in the EP on this topic started in 2013. The first steps were taken in 2015, while the first important results were obtained in 2018, the main protagonist being DG INLO. Three factors have prompted reflection on a new conception of space in parliamentary workplaces:

- the need to reduce expenses and to organise buildings on the basis of less available space
- the generalised disruption posed by digital technologies as a work tool, a new eWorld
- the arrival of a new generation of staff that does not like working in closed spaces, does not like being relegated to solitude in a closed office, which instead loves contact and mobility.

These three factors have led to a global revision of the way workplaces are organised, not only in private but also in public institutions, both European and international: this is why the EP has committed itself to this path. Again, as was to be expected there was no shortage of defenders of the traditional approach, with its long corridors and separate and closed offices: it must be said that in large part this reaction was directed at the hypothesis of having large open spaces without assigning an individual workplace and without fixed work tools. The EP, after an extensive and in-depth assessment, has adopted a solution that I think is both intelligent and balanced, in the knowledge that the management of space and facilities is at the heart of what I have previously called the administrative ecosystem. In the working space, there are factors at play like financial savings, the modernisation of the work tools and the personal satisfaction of the staff, both from a psychological and career viewpoint, which are essential to the quality of their working life. This intelligent and balanced solution consists of the following elements:

a) open spaces are not generalised, they are actually a rather limited solution and largely on a voluntary basis, with a certain number of square metres guaranteed per person;

a-bis) in open spaces, however, each member of staff has their own desk and their own desk-devices;

b) a number of collaborative spaces have been created, where colleagues can meet to exchange opinions or work information on a spontaneous basis;

c) there are also (numerous) social corners where colleagues can meet for relaxing exchanges, not necessarily professional in nature;

d) often not far from these social corners there are small kitchens available to all, fresh water dispensers, and vending machines for various products;

e) obviously there are meeting rooms with video conferencing, which can be used according to a booking calendar.

These solutions have changed the atmosphere of the workplace, have generally been well received and are starting to be developed even more, thanks to the balance that underlies them. At the end of the day, then, integrating people, tools and space is a cultural thing[3], because it involves the global attitude of people.

Changing the workplace has affected, in recent years, also the offices of Members, following pressure from them due to the conceptual (and sometimes even material) obsolescence of the facilities available: this was a phenomenon without distinction between young or old, women or men. The main request was the need for flexibility in office supplies that could be adapted to the needs of MEPs and their closest collaborators. After a long preparation phase, including discussions and a search for legal solutions, this need was also met, through a change in the concept of procurement and more dynamic and varied purchases.

---

[3]G. Ravasi, *#L'Umanità*, reminds us of Mafalda's affirmation that "to love humanity is not a great effort: it's loving the man next door" (Quino) to which Linus replies from afar with "I love humanity... it's people I can't stand" (Charles Schultz). Using these quotations as a basis, G. Ravasi says "I have drawn the acute critique of love for the next one bandied about by many, provided that this next one is not your very level-headed business colleague..." (La Domenica Sole-24Ore on 27 January 2019).

In the second half of the 8th parliamentary term, the EP launched a reflection on covering thirty years of real estate policy. In the meantime, the two solutions adopted can be consolidated, one for the staff inspired by balance, the other for the MEPs inspired by flexibility: both solutions are perfectly in harmony with a work-based approach inspired by a highest levels of mobility, connectivity and interoperability. Mobility means enabling people to work (or interact) anywhere, and also (if not above all) when on the move. Connectivity means that all of the information and documentation needed for parliamentary work must be accessible away from the EP's premises. Interoperability means being able to exchange documents with other institutions, or other political and administrative players without technical difficulties.

The point to remember is that it is not just a matter of introducing new tools into a traditional working environment, but rather it is about evolving towards a new method of working, which means new approaches in both space (buildings, offices, places of work) and time (travelling, remote, teleworking). Integrating all these elements within one homogenous vision will be decisive in the configuration of the future Parliament.

I therefore want to go a little further with this analysis and look at where the relationship with spaces is born, because this relationship is not just about management. Today, this is a fact, we work in a space characterized by a high level of technology. Helping to understand better comes from applying neuroscience to architecture and to organisation[4].

First, for architecture, the following sentence is particularly revealing: "When we enter a Gothic cathedral, the spirit leaps along the high arches. If we go through a dark tunnel we feel threatened and oppressed. When we walk on a boardwalk we feel a sense of lightness. These are intuitive experiences centred on the interaction

---

[4]Psychoanalysis is also worth remembering: from this point of view, an important book that helps understand the dynamics that are grafted in the workplace, the problems that derive from it and how to face them is S. Allcorn and H.F. Stein, *The Dysfunctional Workplace. Theory, Stories and Practices*, University of Missouri Press, Columbia, 2015; the book adopts an essentially psychoanalytic approach and examines case studies to which managerial solutions are proposed.

between us humans and the space in which we live[5]". So it is not just about well-being but about feelings related to precognitive expectations that activate areas of the sensory-motor cortex. Architecture identifies metaphors (like dynamism, lightness, relaxation) and translates them into spaces by playing with light, materials, geometry, topology, and more: the results and impacts are extraordinary on learning speed, level of absenteeism, use of medicines and so on. It is evident that open common and shared spaces lend themselves better to these interventions much more than individual closed spaces. If, in addition, we also wanted to resort to psycho-pedagogy, we would discover that social osmosis produces learning and that knowing how to "argue" (discuss) eliminates violence: this is what is called collaborative learning[6].

Applying neurosciences to organisation today plays an important role because of the use of new technologies as work (and life) tools: the two central problems concern complex texts and memorisation, both of which are very weakened by the frequent use of technology tools and online communication. Using them leads to information bombardment that promotes fragmented and fast reading and inattention, which in turn leads to loss of memorisation that can have a significant impact on organisation.[7] But what has been defined as "the loss of cognitive patience"[8] is particularly delicate: the spasmodic style of online reading risks transferring to all readings and therefore prevents immersion in challenging texts, empathy with the text and

---

[5]This fantastic passage comes from an article by A. Maccaferri, *L'empatia degli spazi accresce produttività e qualità della vita*, in Domenica 24-Ore,18 Novembre 2018. It was this article that prompted me to look deeper into the issue: that is why I did an online search starting with the Tuned project mentioned in the article (tuned-arch.it/home.html) and from there looked into various related topics, learning what I share in the text.

[6]See the interview by M. Croci of Daniele Novara, president of the CPP (Centro PsicoPedagogico for education and conflict management), published by Sette - Corriere della Sera on 6 December 2018. Also see Dan Pontefract, *Learning by osmosis* in https://www.danpontefract.com/learning-by-osmosis/

[7]L. Pronzato, in Liberi Tutti on 18 January 2019, reports numerous examples of people dealing with these problems and the solutions they have adopted to overcome them.

[8]M. Wolf, *Lettore vieni a casa. Il cervello che legge in un mondo digitale*, Edition Vita e Pensiero, Milan, 2018.

critical analysis of it.[9]

These studies cannot be ignored when it comes to the organisational development of the EPA and the working life of staff. Obviously, the life "external" from the workplace, where online technology is the same (if not more) dominant, has a big influence on individual behaviour. It is for this reason that we must create balanced conditions and favour what neuroscience defines as "bi-literacy" within the EP.

---

[9]Ibidem

Chapter 5

Management and Knowledge Sharing

In the previous chapters we have seen how planning method, innovative tools and new approach to working are essential to equipping parliamentary administration with the instruments needed to respond to a society (citizens, businesses, organisations, etc) that is more and more politically demanding and technologically advanced. We have also seen that the access to documents, the use of open data, the transparency requests, the network participation, are all elements that foreshadow a type of e-Democracy that the Parliament cannot afford to ignore today[1]. Indeed, the management does not concern only budget, staff and objectives, but it concerns also complexity, diversity, uncertainty and, most of all, expectations coming from MEPs, staff and citizens.

In January 2018, as previously mentioned, an EP Administration Innovation Day was organised. There is an important lesson to retain from this initiative[2]: while most of the projects presented will use a technological solution, innovative working is not merely about the

---

[1] K. Welle (editor), *100 steps forward etc. cit.;* G.Vilella, *E-Democracy etc. cit.*.

[2] The EPA Innovation Day on 11 January 2019 has, from this point of view, adopted, confirmed and consolidated the same approach.

technological solution[3]. Technology definitely supports and enables the innovative ideas about cooperation, communication, knowledge sharing and many other aspects of our organisation. With mainstreaming innovation, we have an opportunity to capitalise on any innovative ideas to transform incrementally our ways of working across the EP. This also enables and promotes a culture of innovation and empowers any "innovator" to make proposals and receive support in developing innovative solutions that will change our ways of working in various domains. All these elements are essential to improving time management and have largely been metabolised by the EP: the measures taken have certainly reinforced two fundamental aspects of good management, that is, vision and decision.

However, all these aspects do not exhaust the issue of what management is necessary for the Parliament of the future. There are many other elements to be considered such as problem solving approach, participative innovation and empathy[4], as well as especially security concerns, financial regulation and civil service charter (Staff Regulation), risks evaluation and internal audit: all these elements impose obligations that must be taken into account. Let's consider them one by one.

The impact of personnel management on management as a whole is particularly important, especially taking into account the planning approach. However, we must always bear in mind the context in which we find ourselves: for years now, Member States made a constant pressure to change the conditions of the European Civil Service, both from a financial point of view and from an organisational point of view. This pressure produces permanent tension and eliminates the sense of stability that would be necessary for good management. Such external pressure is favoured by the "political" context I mentioned at the beginning of this study: if the EU is seen as an elite, its administration is associated with this judgment, and if Euroscepticism grows, it also

---

[3]As said by I. Ortenzi in *Innovation manager*, etc. cit., innovation is the meeting point between new idea, situation and technology, and is transformed into a project inspired by the values of the organisation.

[4]M. Garcia, N. de Peganow, *Innovation participative*, Èdition Scrineo, Paris 2012; J. Fox, *Comment être un bon manager*, Archipoche, Paris 2004 ; D.W. Bijl, *The New Way of Working*, Parcc, Zeewolde 2011.

builds antipathy towards the European public service. Again: all this undermines the stability within which the staff is managed. Nevertheless, staff management remains a particularly important aspect of an administration that wants to base its activities on vision and planning. This approach, in fact, should be able to determine which staff you need both for the implementation of the adopted projects and for the strategy that looks towards the future: the general trend determined by strategy and planning is certainly that of increasing the qualified personnel, by (essentially) reversing the ratio between AST and AD in favour of the latter. However, defining which qualified professional skills are necessary[5] is a delicate and complicated exercise, taking into account the process of reducing the organisation chart.

When it comes to personnel management, there is an important actor that needs to be taken into account, both because it has an institutionalised role and because it expresses the feelings of a part of the staff: the Staff Committee, made up of staff-elected representatives. In general terms (i.e. independently of the EP) the points of view on how such an organ should act, along the line that goes from conflict to collaboration, can be and in reality are very different, but also changing according to the given conditions: one thing, however, is valid in all circumstances and that is that good management must not ignore the requests (even if not shared) made by such an organ. In fact, even the contents (I mean the framework) of the exchanges of opinions between management and staff committees should be clear for both parties. In theory it should be a discussion on the principles that regulate the management that remains the responsibility of the management of the institution, but often it becomes an examination of specific or even individual cases.

This is why I thought it essential to the analysis contained in this study to take on board the observations of the Bureau of the Staff Committee, in a list that holds certain importance and which I report on below, because it is interesting for my analysis to understand which

---

[5]The book by F. Caselli, *Technology differences* etc. cit. emphasises the difference between skilled workers and unskilled workers: the abundance of the former and their efficient use clearly constitute a considerable advantage.

are the essential points on which to open the comparison[6]. Creating and consolidating a climate of trust between personnel and administration appears to be a priority in these observations. To do this, according the Staff Committee Bureau, we should focus on (at least) some central actions: a) the resources made available to staff must be more developed; b) decisions made in regard to complaints must be clear and precise; c) access to documents (in personnel management) must be guaranteed and even the simple document searches on the Intranet should be facilitated; d) finally, if there is an intervention by the Ombudsman, the recommendations should be applied in full. Besides these actions, which are linked to the solidity of trust, there are other concerns that seem to me interesting when reflecting on good management. The first is that we should keep a historical memory of the choices made in personnel policy, in order to link it to the need for homogeneous staff treatment, which has been put under pressure by uncoordinated decentralisation or lack of interinstitutional collaboration. On a more tangible level, strategic choices such as teleworking, mobility and project activities need prior staff training to be successful and effective.

The impact of financial regulation on management is also important. In this respect, it must be kept in mind that the strategic vision of the administration does not always coincide with the political outlook when it comes to financial decision-making processes. It is not that there is a clear separation, especially since agreement at political level is sometimes necessary to adopt the strategies of the administration, but certainly there is a décalage due to the needs of political action that has at most an annual budget-linked perspective. The financial sector, in fact, although by its nature is subjected to at least annual planning, is in concrete adapted to a fragmentary model, where decisions are made on the basis of real facts or of accumulation of ideas that arise from incidental facts. Just one example among many, is a large project like the Parlamentarium. That experience means we un-

---

[6]I met the Staff Committee Bureau before the start of the study: any inaccuracy that may be contained in the comments that follow is attributable only to me. In my opinion, these are pertinent and interesting observations which I refer to in the chapter on perspectives.

derstand that it is also useful to open a Museum of European History, and then on the basis of the new experience acquired it is clear that a house dedicated to the "stories" of Europeans would be a valid action for citizens. The political decision-making process can therefore be fragmented and built on the accumulation of ideas, but financial management allows positive answers to these requests thanks to the margins of manoeuvre created by the new savings (reduction of personnel and access to real estate) and from the practice of ramassage. It seems clear that the timing of the political decision may require a high degree of flexibility with regard to financial management: but this flexibility is possible paradoxically thanks to a clear strategic vision on the part of the administration on how to manage the resources and how to create the necessary room for manoeuvre. This is not the case, however, for the administration's own projects that need a clear planning in order to be implemented: indeed, to be precise, only clear planning of the administration's projects allows intelligent management of the margins necessary for political flexibility.

The construction of a system that includes a Risk Manager, a Business Continuity Management and an Internal Auditor helps to frame the administration's activity within the context of permanent and global scrutiny, aimed at supporting and protecting the quality of work[7]. These transversal activities are all part of a single assurance framework that impacts our daily actions: quickly channeling information and coordinating information flows with our EP authorities has become a necessity in view of the increasing attention given inside the EP to assurance and performance information.

The Internal Auditor (IAS) has played a very important and particular role during these years, also considering that the Risk Manager and the Business Continuity Management are newly established (after a long period of gestation) and reconstituted (after a long period of hibernation), respectively. IAS has created added value thanks to its approach based on a clear vision of its role: proposals inspired by

---

[7]The book by H. Kerzner, *Project Management, Metrics, KPIs and Dashboards. A Guide to Measuring and Monitoring Project Performance*, Wiley New York, 2017, is very important in understanding the foundations of this homogeneous sector and adopting the most pertinent measures for its solid construction.

a homogeneous logic were the result, although they differ in content depending on the recipients. By studying both the general and sectorial reports produced in the last few years by the IAS, it is possible to highlight a key point: the "governance" of the sector in question is always the key request when it comes to improving management[8].

- Governance, again according to IAS reports, must be accompanied by a business strategy,
- a related programme,
- a risk assessment
- and a correct allocation of resources, especially human resources. It is also logical to clarify responsibilities regarding the implementation of the necessary actions.

The IAS, although this is a recent evolution, arises not as a pure controller but as an actor ready to help, if required, in the implementation phase, essentially with continuous reporting that follows the evolution of activities. This step forward has, more recently, led to more mutual trust and bilateral respect between the Auditor and the administration, which are conditions necessary for the success of the activities. In short, IAS should not be seen as an administrative burden or as something that only wants to seek out flaws, but as an opportunity for the manager of each level - medium, senior, top - to revisit their working methods.

The introduction of the KPI (key performance indicators) goes in the same direction: on theoretical basis the KPI can be used for daily/weekly directing activities, monthly operating review, quarterly performance review or annual strategic planning guidance, they can be presented to employees for incentivising and/or presented to investors and suppliers (that correspond, *mutatis mutandi*, to the political level for the EP)[9]. This exercise promotes the development of a

---

[8]A seminar at the European University Institute was dedicated to the importance of establishing governance mechanisms, when needed at a political and administrative level, in all sectors: *Challenges to Governance beyond the State*, held at Fiesole on 10 ottobre 2018 (speakers: M. Galeotti, D. Toshkov, O. Westerwinter). On the global level, however, we can see experiences of governance in cooperation between the public and private sectors.

[9]C. Pennell, *Maturity in Government Digital Transformation Journeys*, September 2018. Once again, the book by H. Kerzner, *Project Management*,

comprehensive framework of operational performance objectives that enable, both in the planning and reporting activities, to use a common language across a diversity of services and professional specialisations.

Last, but not least we need to mention the impact of security on management, as a new phenomenon. The spread of terrorism over the last few years around the world and in particular in Europe has imposed security problems everywhere and on everyone, leading to consequences for logistics, behaviour and (therefore) activities: this also applies to the European Parliament, where indeed the problem is amplified by the fact it is an "open" institution by vocation. The impact on management has been considerable. The administration's approach has been oriented along three lines, strictly linked to sound management:

– introducing a culture of safety,
– fostering awareness of the problem at all levels,
– and creating a feeling of reciprocity in dealing with problems. and solving them through good cooperation.

These are choices that include the involvement of all the management in order to be successful, and it is important that they succeed because only in this way the EP can maintain its vocation as an open institution and continue (as has actually been done!) to offer new services to the public instead of scaling them back. Of course, that is without mentioning the continuation and guaranteeing of the institutional political activity of MEPs, even in moments of greater tension. But there is another impact on the management's plan: it is that, by having security assume a certain importance, even a real dignity, the professions linked to it have made a leap forward in quality, and they have been inserted, with attached legal provisions, fully in the scheme of the parliamentary public function, creating new balances. Now: all these measures (action lines, managerial cooperation, new professionalism, confirmation of open vocation) have greatly benefited from the approach of a strategic vision that has been implemented through planning.

So, to sum up, the element to keep firmly in mind in the reflections that follow is thus: an administrative policy that, based on

---

Metrics, KPIs etc. cit. is of big help in defining this sector.

vision and strategy, points to a permanent innovation process cannot be, and is not, a pure theoretical and philosophical abstraction. It must take into account, rather, incorporate, the "classic" aspects of management such as personnel management, financial management, risk assessment and, nowadays, safety and security. Each of these factors must be incorporated by taking into account its specificities, determined by economic context, then subject to evolution.

Chapter 6

Consequences of EPA Approach

Reforming the administration and management is by no mean an impromptu invention of the European Parliament and its Secretary General: it has been on the radars of public institutions for some decades, supported by theoretical and academic research[1]. One of the most solid concepts that has emerged in recent years, but which is still valid today, is that of "capacity building". It includes quality of management, openness, long-term orientation, continuous improvement and quality of workforce: setting a strategic framework (mission, vision, values) must be followed, always, by monitoring, evaluation and learning, that at the end leads to the management of quality[2]. All this is comprehended in the international standard ISO 9001-2008 where engagement of top management, vision and measurement are three of the key pillars of the QMS[3]. Another aspect that has been in the spotlight for at least thirty years in the processes of management and management reform is the adoption of essential principles and val-

---

[1] See C. Pollitt-G. Bouckaert, *Public Management Reform. A Comparative Analysis*, Oxford University Press, Oxford, 2011.

[2] Compare with R. Maconick - P. Morgan, *Capacity-building supported by the United Nations*, United Nations Editions, 1999 and A. De Waal, *The Secret of High performance Organizations*, Management Online Review, April, 2010.

[3] B.G. Dale – T. van der Wiele – T. van Iwaarden, *Managing Quality*, Wiley-Blackwell, Oxford, 2007.

ues, which are valid in general terms. An amalgam list of European principles and values fundamental for a good public administration is as follows: legality, integrity, impartiality, inclusiveness, openness, user-centricity, responsiveness, connectivity, efficiency, effectiveness, sustainability, vision, reflection, innovation, accountability[4].

What is peculiar about the EPA's recent approach is that the reform process, which contains the principles and international standard mentioned above, is characterised by a strong willing of innovation changes[5]. Indeed, on the basis of the present study analysis I can certainly say that the EP administration – thanks to the several steps of its last ten years' transformational journey - is a modern organisation developing a managerial mindset, looking for innovative solutions and oriented towards a technological approach: the strongest pillar of this modernity appears to be the strategic "Vision", on which the EP administration has very much invested, in the meaning that any action must be permanently a step of a defined way.

What are, therefore, the results that I think should be drawn from the analysis conducted up to this point[6]? I intend to talk about the

---

[4]The list, in the order indicated and with an explanation for each of the concepts, is included in the European Commission's, *Quality of Public Administration. A Toolbox for practitioners*, Luxembourg, European Union, 2015, p. 21-23. The Toolbox aims to support and inspire innovators of public administration and brings together almost 170 case studies as "inspiring examples" (better concept than the old "best practices"). Many of these principles and values have also been included in the *Charter of good administrative behaviour*, adopted by the European Ombudsman.

[5]On the absolute need to create fundamental organisational changes in order to keep up with the needs of the contemporary world, see the work of J. Beckford, *The Intelligent Organization*, Routledge, London, 2016. The term "Intelligent" means able to initiate or modify actions in the light of ongoing events: on this basis, the book focuses not only on the transformation of performance but also on the capitalisation of potential.

[6]I would like to point out that the reflections and proposals that follow concern only the methodological level, which is the purpose of this study. The practical proposals of administrative structures could possibly derive from methodological reflections. To give two concrete examples: Internal Mediation is a solution explored but never adopted by the EP, but which I believe should be taken seriously into consideration. An organisational solution optimised by the European Commission *Toolbox* is the One-stop-shop (OSS) that the EP has also adopted internally: it's an instrument that should be developed. And so on. All this relates

consequences and results (in this chapter) that will help us to open a pathway for the future (next chapter).

The first important consequence is that vision implies changes[7].

The EP is certainly ready for changes and is preparing to change: transform management, foster innovation, share responsibilities. Implementing changes is always a challenge, and if changes are permanent you need high level of agility. The process cannot stop, change and innovate is a philosophy that needs fresh thinking: however, with changes people are called to abandon their comfort zone and this can create panic; only thanks to a process of learning we could reach a magic zone where changes are welcome and desirable[8]. But, systematising transformation helps to consolidate it, then I think that one adjustment that must be done is the following: you also need steps for giving the organisation the capacity to continue absorbing previous changes.

Let's go ahead with consequences.

Self-projection towards the future is a continuous exercise that cannot stop at the management level (middle to top management): it needs to enlarge and create link and alignment between the strategic vision and the operational level, by increasing awareness and engagement of the latter and reciprocal trust[9]. On the basis of clarity on goals, I think that we have to adopt an inclusive approach with operational level that engages it in a shared responsibility framework. It means that exchange best practices should be the normal way of interacting amongst services: this implies openness as a fundamental factor to fostering modernity.

Let's go ahead.

Human ideas grow faster in an environment where collaboration

---

to a (possible) next phase of the discussion.

[7]I. Ortenzi, *Innovation manager*, etc. cit. reminds us that innovation changes behaviour and habits and, in this way, generates values.

[8]A similar approach (with some differences from my proposal) that confirms the importance of the issue, can be found in E.C. *Quality of Public Administration. A Toolbox etc. cit, p. 175.* the cascade list is shock, denial, realisation, acceptance, experimentation, understanding, integration.

[9]Frances Frei *(Harvard Business School), How to build (and rebuild) trust,* Ted Talk, 4 May 2018 (YouTube).

and shared information is fostered. But that is not enough and it is
necessary to go even further. Recent scientific studies have shown the
significant importance of cooperation, which must be distinguished
from collaboration[10]. Today it is clear that: collaboration concerns
the operational level, while cooperation calls for all human capabilities
and goals. Collaboration (as an operational factor) is determined
by time, while cooperation has bigger horizons; collaboration is on a
certain object, while cooperation is a continuous process of knowledge-
sharing[11]. A lack of cooperation, in the sense now indicated, produces
nervousness and instability, and therefore an incapacity to adapt to
innovation.

This requires openness in the exchange of information and a culture of cooperation that puts the end-user at the centre. It is essential
to frame the concept of internal cooperation taking into account the
EPA journey accomplished so far: without a definitive improvement
in our capacity to cooperate on complex processes, we will fail to grasp
challenges and opportunities. But most of all, as complexity will increase, the lack of internal cooperation will bring the risk weaken
our corporate dimension: this is the reason why internal cooperation
has to be understood first of all as a collective responsibility and engagement. For it to be effective, internal cooperation needs to find a
proper place both in the processes and in the structure of the organisation: sometimes, the blocking factor is to be found in conflicting
priorities that fail to consider the biggest picture, the sum of local
optimisations never equals a corporate success.

So: exchange practices and sharing responsibility means to increase and consolidate a corporate and cooperative culture in order
to overcome silos[12]. The illusion of self-sufficiency and habit of looking

---

[10]E. Laurent,*L'impasse collaborative*, Les liens qui libèrent, Paris, 2018. An
important and almost symbolic piece of information to note for my study on the
EP is that the author, prof. Laurent, teaches at Science Po Paris and at Stanford
University!

[11]This analysis is put forward by E. Laurent,*L'impasse collaborative*, etc. cit. It
should be noted that the author makes a philosophical analysis of modern societies,
but shows the concrete repercussions on the economy and on organisations.

[12]On this specific aspect it is useful to consult M. Benedick-R. Collart, *Bâtir
une organisation collaborative*, Pearson France, Montreuil, 2018: the book focuses
(as a sort of manual) on collaborative managerial practices, such as turn-based

inward do not have a place anymore in our administration. However, two practical conditions must be met to reshape EP internal cooperation: share our vision and objectives even more, take the necessary time for it and never give it for granted, and accept the necessary flexibility for reaching our objectives. This can successfully happen only with a strong commitment from the top management and with a generally values-based management.

It means that everybody's participation is essential[13]. Contributing to the common objectives through one's own role and responsibilities is even more important. To enable everybody's participation, the process of consultation must be genuine, concrete and sincere. Only through this process can we ensure that listening is made on an equal foot. This way, we look for the right solutions. On the contrary, thinking we are always right and already have the solution will never trigger a fruitful consultation process: the other's attention will never be gained like that. The consultation should lead to decisions supporting the right solutions to reach a common objective. Only in that logic can a decision make sense for everybody. Giving orders for the sake of it without leaving margins for interpretation simply does not work in complex, professional organisations such as EP.

Another important consequence to be drawn concerns the programmatic approach to activities: this is certainly a very positive method that must be maintained. It is necessary to continue (more than in the past) to analyse policy content in order to support managerial choices and to repeat the analysis of perspectives regularly, as a basis for planning. The latter is brought about through projects, and we must continue (even more than in the past) to put emphasis on corporate projects, in strategic issues within the scope of a common goal. In this context we must not forget the institutional obligations that reappear regularly (State of Union, Legislative Work

---

leadership, decision by agreement, ecosystem creation, animation and then give substance through the concrete experiences of various companies, using interviews as well. However, for a complete view on the concept of knowledge sharing I suggest to see A. Styhre, *Knowledge Sharing in Professions*, Gower Limited, Burlington, 2011, and also N. Holden and M. Glisby, *Creating Knowledge Advantage*, Copenhagen Business School Press, Copenhagen, 2010.

[13]M. Garcia, N. de Peganow, *Innovation participative*, etc. cit.

Programme, Budget, etc.) and which should influence the planning.

One important correction that is required, however, is to eliminate excess planning, to reduce the number of projects that have become exorbitant. This hypertrophy of project management throughout the EP will impact the daily work: finding a balance between too many and too few projects, too small and too big projects is a priority, taking also into account that every complex project should have an acceptable lifecycle, say 3 to 5 years[14], to be credible. Hyperprojectuality is creating problems that will lead to paralysis, in a situation in which the plan can no longer be sustainable because of an objective inability to cope with exorbitant requests.

This requires an adjustment that, to me, seem necessary: accepting requests in order to have wider margins of flexibility. Tightening, closing and forcing all activity into the planning is not needed: leaving important margins of flexibility and spontaneous creativity to cope with situations helps the operational level. It is by providing the direction and the expected result that a professional organisation can best use its technical capacity with the necessary flexibility for execution. Giving straight orders is the last resort, because management has to answer to the need for results.

A further consequence that we can draw is that the scrutiny system must be strengthened thanks to the introduction of a cultural change: delays in the implementation of a project should not be perceived in itself as a negative fact. The good implementation of a project (or a programme) is subject to review and reflection, to lessons learned and adaptation: systematic monitoring planning and managing evaluations together with the growing role of performance audits can assess whether the implementation is progressing[15]. Reforming administration and management is a means to multiple ends, one of those is freeing officials from constraints that inhibit their action for supporting the political accountability: this is why performance management is now taken extremely seriously[16]. Therefore, we must

---

[14]L. Délépine et al.,*IT Governance Hub*, Brussels, August, 2018

[15]Cfr. E.C. *Quality of Public Administration. A Toolbox etc. cit, p. 73.*

[16]G. Bouckaert – J. Halligan, *Managing Performance: International Comparison*, Routledge, London, 2008

conclude that meetings as collegial monitoring and evaluation, the risk management control system and IAS activity should not be seen as an administrative burden to be handled but as an opportunity for managers of every level - be it medium, senior or top - to review their working methods.

Furthermore, the clarity and simplicity of the rules applicable within an organisation is a fundamental factor that allows for correct managerial management. Regular review and simplification should be carried out regularly, at least once a year, and should be tasked to a specific entity, also with the aim of reducing regulatory burdens at operational level and for users of the administration's services.

Finally, we have to remember that all this is achieved not only in time, but also in space. We should have well in mind that staff motivation has to do with environment where we work every day, the workplace must be a desirable place to stay. The workplace must support talent, engagement and cooperation with the help of new technologies: digital and flexibility are the essential factors, bypassing the obsolete debate on open space versus offices.

These are the effects that I have drawn from the analysis conducted in this study and these effects support the perspective reflections that follow. I think that that is why it is very useful to make a brief summary, showing the logical (and cascade) structure of my construction:

- vision implies changes: give the organisation the capacity to continue absorbing previous changes
- vision is a continuous exercise: exchange best practices should be the normal way of interacting amongst services
- interacting amongst services: collaborate on projects but cooperate on strategy
- consolidate a corporate and cooperative culture: everybody's participation is essential, share our vision and objectives at all level
- programmatic approach to activities is fundamental: avoid excess planning
- checking risks: introduce a cultural change, control should not be seen as an administrative burden but as an opportunity

– clarity and simplicity of the internal rules is a fundamental factor: make regular review
– staff motivation has to do with the environment where we work every day: the workplace must be a desirable place to stay.

Chapter 7

Possible Perspectives

At this point, it is appropriate to ask the following basic question: why is having clear vision and planning such an important thing for an organisation? The body of literature is immense, both bibliographic and webliographic, so it is my responsibility to choose those that seem the most relevant to our case.

First, let us consider Vision.

Vision provides unanimity of purpose and gives a sense of belonging to the employees, serve as focal point to identify themselves, provides a philosophy of existence to the employees (Management Study Guide[1]).

A clear Vision acts as a unifying force, a guide for employees actions, a factor for motivating and inspiring (Cornerstone Dynamics[2]).

Vision allows organisations to be proactive rather than reactive, to foresee their future and prepare accordingly, to increase operational efficiency (Envisio[3]).

We could go on for a long time, but these already seem to me sound enough reasons to confirm the importance of having a Vision: I would just like to add that future projections must be memorable

---

[1]https://www.managementstudyguide.com/importance-of-vision-and-mission-statements.htm

[2]https://www.cornerstonedynamics.com/3-big-benefits-of-a-clear-vision-statement/

[3]https://www.envisio.com/blog/benefits-of-strategic-planning

thanks to concise sentences that have a real impact on the whole staff. And even more, in a complex, polyphonic environment such as the EPA, Vision provides a common language through which cooperation and collaboration can materialize.

Next, Planning.

Planning breaks down silos in favour of a holistic perspective; provides possibility to think and talk openly; increases the value of staff; provides a framework to ask questions; ensures working on the right things; bring order; uncovers new ideas; achieves alignment of team; determines agreement on priorities; establishes accountability (Greg Bustin[4]).

Planning gives the organisation a sense of direction; focuses on objectives and results; establishes basis for teamwork; helps anticipate problems; provides guidelines for decisions; and serves as a prerequisite of a good management (Cliffsnotes[5]).

Planning helps achieve savings; facilitates controlling; encourages innovation; minimises uncertainties; facilitates coordination; improves staff moral (Management Study Guide[6]).

Once again, we could go on with Planning, but even then I think the reasons listed are sufficiently strong to confirm the importance of procedures based on planning: we just have to add that the planning process should always start with the evaluation of the resources available to the organisation. As a result, it is necessary to link the planning to the budget forecasts and to the staffing forecasts, and then report the results in the RAA (activity annual report). It would also be important to do the planning exercise on a regular basis, setting a specific time (a proper calendar) of year for it.

An organisation (as is the case with the EPA) that wants to base its activities on Vision and Planning absolutely needs to clarify and develop another couple of concepts, Metrics and Matrix: both are indeed essential to setting a course towards projects and programme,

---

[4]https://bustin.com/executive-leadership-blog/why_bother_10_benefits_of_planning/

[5]https://www.cliffsnotes.com/study-guides/principles-of-management

[6]https://www.managementstudyguide.com/planning_advantages.htm

especially when it is based on common goals, in a corporate approach. That is why we undergo the same exercise as above, asking ourselves what are the advantages of adopting the Metrics method and the Matrix method, respectively.

First, Matrix.
Matrix management brings together managers and employees from different departments to collaborate with each other towards the accomplishment of the organizational goals. The following are some of the advantages of matrix management: Effective Communication of Information; Efficient Use of Resources; Increased Motivation; Flexibility; Skills Development; Discipline Retention (Denizon Team[7]).

Matrix organization is a type of organizational structure which facilitates a horizontal flow of skills and informations, mainly applied in large projects. The matrix organizational structure brings the employees and managers together to work on a specific goal. Using matrix organization structure would: improve the ability to access all the resources; enhance coordination across the organization; give faster decentralized decisions; improve access to diverse range of skills and perspectives of the employees and the managers; provide more multi-skilled workers; and lastly increase communication and coordination across the business (Management Square[8]).

The cardinal advantage of a matrix structure is that it facilitates rapid response to change in two or more environments. Matrix structures are flatter and more responsive than other types of structures because they permit more efficient exchanges of information. In addition to speed and flexibility, matrix organization may result in a more efficient use of resources than other organic structures. Other benefits of matrix management include improved motivation and more adept managers (D. Mote, Encyclopedia for business[9]).

As you can see, there is a wide convergence between the benefits produced by the adoption of the Matrix method. However, one

---

[7]https://www.denizon.com/operational-efficiency-initiatives/matrix-management-benefits-and-pitfalls/

[8]https://www.management-square.com/matrix-organization/

[9]https://www.referenceforbusiness.com/encyclopedia/Man-Mix/Matrix-Management-and-Structure.html

should not forget that precisely because of its atypical characteristics, this method comes with risks that have to be avoided in order to prevent a mechanism block. These risks could include tension (if not full-blown conflict) between managers, confusion among operating staff and possible internal organisation complexities. The Matrix approach, however, is certainly the most efficient instrument for making the organisation adapt to working on strategic projects.

Now, Metrics

Metrics are numbers that tell you important information about a process under review. They tell you accurate measurements about how the process is functioning and provide base for you to suggest improvements. Here are some important functions that metrics fulfil in an organization: Control and Feedback Loop is Driven by Metrics; Metrics Make the Process Objective; Improvement Goals are in Terms of Metrics (MSG Management Guide[10]).

Metrics drive your operating model. Metrics clarify performance expectations. Metrics drive business execution. Metrics focus people's attention on what is important. Metrics help you run more effective meetings. Metrics help you to hold people accountable. (S. Lynch[11]).

Metrics are used to drive improvements and help businesses focus their people and resources on what's important. Good metrics will: Drive the strategy and direction of the organization; Provide focus for an organization, department or employee; Help make decisions; Drive performance; Change and evolve with the organization; Produce good internal and external public relations (G. Forrest[12]).

The importance of Metrics is therefore quite evident, but in this case also we must not forget the risks. The main one is perceiving the Metrics method as a pure and simple control mechanism, which is all-seeing and cumbersome. These considerations can lead to criticism about its suitability for this and that activity. The second risk is equally important to bear in mind: Metrics tend to spill over into

---

[10]https://www.managementstudyguide.com/what-are-metrics.htm

[11]https://www.linkedin.com/pulse/benefits-having-right-kpis-key-performance-indicators-stephen-lynch

[12]https://www.isixsigma.com/implementation/basics/importance-implementing-effective-metrics/

the domain of the Matrix, weakening and impeding the latter proper development. It is therefore essential in the near future to position Metrics and Matrix in such a way that they are balanced and can consolidate the method of working set out in Vision and Planning.

Since the beginning of his mandate, the Secretary General Klaus Welle has been looking for a project with which everyone could identify, bearing in mind future prospects that could be scheduled, in the belief that this could change the behaviour of staff members. His great merit in the first stages of the EPA transformational journey was to have continued determinedly not only against opponents, but also when faced by those who welcomed these ideas with only polite irony, and developed his actions during ten years. This study and its results allow me to say that we must continue to follow the path open ahead of us to its end and, in addition, that we can obtain further and much more advanced results. This will create an EPA that will be a reference point for all the institutions, but also a resilient organization able to deliver results in troubled times.

After analysing the work experience of the parliamentary administration over the last ten years from various points of view (planning, matrix, technology, ecosystem, management), and after analysing the consequences of this work, I am able to share outcomes that I consider useful for the future outlook: we need to look at the main factors that will determine whether the path can continue towards higher goals in a sustainable mechanism.

To do so, my proposal is to work along five axes that would consolidate the system:

1. **Simplifying the global model;**
2. **Eliminating hyper-projectuality;**
3. **Merging Metrics and Matrix in a balanced relation**
4. **Substituting scrutiny for hard-control;**
5. **Involving all levels of staff.**

As I have already mentioned (at least a couple of times), the driving force behind the transformational journey of EP administration has been the development and consolidation of the Strategic Vision: from here derive modern and constantly evolving management methods. Reforming the administration is no longer a static act in the

EP, adopted once and for all, but rather a process of constant and permanent innovation. However, (this is the primary result behind my reasoning) such modern methods of permanent innovation that are in continuous evolution must be implemented without excesses of sophistication, that is, they must be immediately comprehensible and accessible. To this end, it seems to me that everything that has been said in this study can be summarised through the following simplified methodological diagram:

Vision ⇒ Planning ⇒ Implementation ⇒ Testing ⇒ Adaptation

Vision should be developed at the level of Top Management as a result of a participatory process, based on a regular analysis of the political context and the new technological tools available.

Planning should be framed within the corporate targets, which derive from the Vision: this implies favouring ambitious projects based on *collaboration* and *cooperation,* while reducing micro-planning, which should be limited to decentralised level. In order to overcome hyper-projectuality we must find a "solution" to break away from old projects that now number in their hundreds: my proposal is not to address the closure of each project, but to make a final report for large groups of projects. Then we could launch "central" (focal) projects in small numbers, which have a long-lasting permanent character and are truly game changers. It is here that using the Matrix method must play a decisive role. This should be completed by a package of training projects that can also maintain a repeated rhythm.

Implementation: this is obviously the central phase, the fulcrum of the whole mechanism and various factors intervene on it. In this study, however, the only methodological element that must be pointed out as relevant for implementation is that the fusion between Metrics and Matrix will be decisive for its ultimate success.

Testing the implementation of the two previous elements must undergo scrutiny at two different levels: firstly, an audit and risk management system serving as added value and support, not as control and judgment; then, a collective process of exchange and comparison. We must avoid that "metrics" become burdensome and even block the apparatus if one considers it as a control mechanism or even as a limitation: the margins of informality are necessary to oil the administrative machine. Professionalising the scrutiny approach enables to grant more flexibility in the implementation process without jeopardising the results.

Adaptation is the next step and, for this reason, leads on to making decisions that make sense for everyone: in this final phase it is necessary to evaluate the organisation's ability to absorb changes. There is a strong "will" and a high degree of determination in pursuing the transformation of the administration when it comes to innovation: that's positive. Sometimes, however, a too strong "determination" leads to bypassing the DGs with which obstacles or problems are encountered, creating parallel paths that produce misunderstandings that are very negative for the administration. Another consequence of a too strong determination is the imposition of limited deadlines, which in turn create dysfunctions. Being able to follow deadlines that allow the involvement of the DGs, advancing step-by-step, is essential to success.

In my opinion, the following scheme (that links the five axes with the methodological diagram) summarises the approach that has been proposed here and lays the foundation for actions that can be used to make adjustments:

Vision: *Simplifying the global model*
⇒ **Planning:** *Eliminating hyper-projectuality*
⇒ **Implementation:** *Merging Metrics and Matrix in a balanced relation*
⇒ **Testing:** *Substituting scrutiny for hard-control*
⇒ **Adaptation:** *Involving all levels of staff.*

This simplified methodological diagram, which amalgamates a decade of experience and possible consequences, frames all the work of the parliamentary administration. The rest are aids that complete and reinforce the methodological diagram: I refer in particular to the exercise of revision and simplification of rules in force, which must be handled on a constant basis. I believe these are the elements that, together, will encourage the consolidation of a true corporate and cooperative culture in our organisation. Which are the concrete actions that should come from the present reflections is an exercise that belongs to a next step.

A Work-Plan

After submitting the final version of this study, the EP Secretary General asked for a list of concrete actions (work-plan) for the implementation of the reflections contained in the present study. The following was my proposal:

1. Brochure for all staff explaining:
   - operation of the Strategy Approach
   - ongoing in-depth insights
2. Roadmap and organisation for regular review of the context and objectives
3. General survey of ongoing projects and decision on:
   - closing
   - abandoning
   - confirming
   - assigning
4. Defining the decentralisation to (enabling) the DGs of:
   - SEF
   - Innovation Day
5. Revisiting the Metrics Method
6. Defining a (true and proper) Matrix Method
7. Redefining KPIs and their use
8. Defining the functioning of the Integrated Scrutiny System
9. Defining a (true and proper) "adaptation" method: absorbing changes
10. Current Management methodology
    - Staff: which staff and which qualified skills
    - Finance: planning for SEF and flexibility at political level
    - Workplace: review of state-of-art and new objectives
    - Rules: review and implementation plan for recommendations
11. Strategic role of technologies and integration between SEF and IT Plan.

Conclusions
Democracy Between Europe and Technology

The administration of the European Parliament, like any other administration of the European institutions, is linked to the general values of the EU and works, within the scope of its duties within the Parliament, towards their realisation. Obviously, talking about the values of the Union would imply a vast analysis, which simply cannot be done here. However, here I must highlight those values that have an immediate impact on administrative (not just political) activity, values that I draw from the Lisbon Treaty and the Berlin (March 2007) and Rome (March 2017) declarations: democracy and the rule of law, peace and freedom, mutual respect and responsibility, prosperity and security, tolerance and participation, justice and solidarity. The key value is clearly that of democracy, of which the EP is the direct expression, and the administration supports the EP's work strengthening democracy. Addressing the whole staff after the 2019 European elections, the EP Secretary General said[13]: *"A historical 51% of citizens voted in the European elections. This is eight percentage points above 2014 and the highest turnout since 1994. I believe this is a real victory for European parliamentary democracy that we should all be proud of... as public servants who believe in the cause of European democracy."*

In this regard, we return to the initial observations of this study

---

[13]Internal Communication *etc. cit.*

and close the circle: as we have seen, there are important challenges that must be taken into account. On the political scene a new approach commonly defined as populist and / or sovereign (nationalist) has imposed itself, bringing with it new questions and new methods: it is now the task of the EP administration to accept the new challenges and work to provide answers, not rely solely on prejudicial rejection that turns out to be ineffective. The question is: how can the working method adopted by the EP help to provide the right answers to these challenges? Vision, planning and quality management must concentrate on these questions and, more precisely, on these objectives. Some useful information comes from a recent in-depth study on the subject, which posed the question of how to govern institutional and organisational change in European administrations[14]. The first great intuition is to understand that the inclusion of citizens in a wider, real multi-level partnership is an essential factor in the solidity of the European administration and, at the same time (through osmosis) of European democracy. The second intuition concerns the usefulness (the necessity) of proceeding with a codification of European administrative law[15], as a further factor for strengthening the organisation (not just the activity). The third intuition is to propose the search for co-administration as a way toward future development of European administrative action. Finally, the study indicates digitization as the main factor that can help strengthen inclusion and other aspects, and therefore democracy.

Indeed, the processes of digitalization of political life and of society as a whole is an important aspect. Alongside the extremely positive factors of this phenomenon there are big problems that undermine democracy, the most important of which is the imbalance that exists in the use of electronic tools: this asymmetry is producing great inequalities among the population and dismay among many

---

[14]A. Monica – G. Balduzzi (ed.), *Governare il cambiamento istituzionale e organizzativo nelle amministrazioni europee*, Pavia University Press, Pavia, 2019, with interesting results and many points of contact with what has been said so far in the present analysis.

[15]The book refers to G. Della Cananea – D.U. Galetta (a cura di*), Codice ReNEUAL del procedimento amministrativo dell'Unione europea*, Editoriale Scientifica, Napoli, 2016.

citizens, who thus seek other "certainties" to lean on[16]. The key word for getting out of this situation is, as has been observed by others[17] "trust": the conditions must be created to foster the growth of citizens' trust in the digital system as a whole. According to the EP Resolution of 16 March 2017[18], there are various aspects that need to be broached in order for e-democracy to be a success, among which I consider the following to be significant: a) the progress of information security and data protection; b) the training of each citizen in the use of new technologies and the elimination of digital literacy gap; c) an adequate communication campaign; d) simplification of languages and procedures in order to make it more understandable; e) ensuring that citizen contributions are incorporated and followed up in decision-making processes. We have to make sure that, although reinforcing the EP to make it a leading player in the digital world is fundamental, we should also encourage the growth of citizens in the use of digital technology. As has been pointedly observed[19], the main factors of change imposed by technologies and relevant to the administration are participation, rights and new actors. Participation is no longer just procedural or testimonial, it now wants to be concrete, real, effective. The administrator is no longer satisfied with "being heard" during an administrative procedure, regardless of the final result, and citizens are no longer satisfied by postponing the showdown to electoral moments. Technology allows both to be constantly present through the various stages of the decision-making process, to learn and verify. Rights are put under pressure by technology and their very essence is questioned, as such they must be redefined or even new ones should emerge. Some substantial examples: the right to privacy, the right to be forgotten, the right to information, all three of these rights today have changed in substance and therefore require a new regulation that cannot aim only to tighten up the

---

[16] A. Baricco, *The Game*, Einaudi, Torino, 2018.

[17] Statement by Professor F. Pizzetti, *GDPR, codice italiano e Data Protection Officer*, conference held at the Università Politecnica delle Marche, Ancona, 8 November 2018.

[18] P8_TA(2017)095 etc. cit.

[19] *Stato e Amministrazione di fronte alla rivoluzione delle ICT: partecipazione, diritti e nuovi attori, etc. cit.*

traditional approach. Finally, new actors appear on the scene and not always in a positive sense: hackers, cyber criminals, cyber espionage, are just a few examples of the problems that must be faced not only through regulation but through the actual repression of illicit activity. Then there are the new technologically-advanced citizens, who want to be protagonists, and there are technological companies that monopolise technical knowledge. But most of all there is a new elite, which originates in the world of technologies and which acquires more and more space, a more and more significant role and more and more influence[20].

The defence of democracy cannot be a static defence, meaning that an immobile and immutable system cannot be defended. Democracy defends itself by developing itself and enlarging its conceptual boundaries, which is facilitated by the appropriation of technology as a normal working tool. Transparency, access to documents, consultation and dialogue are the tools that widen the boundaries of modern democracy by involving citizens: technology is essential to make these tools operational. I could define all that as "Representative Innovation[21]".

However, the purpose of the EP's contribution to the functioning of Democracy is not set in stone, it is a collective everyday effort. As was stated during an important reflection on the forty years of direct election of the European Parliament[22], the EP is itself an actor that contributes decisively to the democratisation of Europe "in

---

[20]A. Baricco, *The Game*, etc. cit.

[21]The term "representative innovation" has been coined by D. Innerarity, *La Democracia en Europa, etc. cit.* although in another context.

[22]I refer to the conference, *40 Years of European Parliament Direct Elections*, held at the European University Institute, Florence, on 22nd - 23rd of November 2018: keynote speaker prof. A. Héritier. Two documents published by the European Parliament were distributed during the conference: the first was prepared by EPRS, Historical Archives Unit, *40th Anniversary of the 1976 Act on Direct Elections to the European Parliament*, EU Luxembourg, 2015, bringing together all the documents from December 1974 to September 1976 that led to the revolutionary decision; the second was prepared by CARDOC, DG PRES, *Towards direct elections to the European Parliament*, European Communities, Luxembourg, 2009, which is a real and legitimate study (author F. Piodi) into the path taken by the European institutions to arrive at the decision.

a political context wherein the legitimacy of the European Union is increasingly contested and Eurosceptic parties seem to gain popularity[23]". We know that in the last decades the EP managed to establish itself as a keystone of the EU's policy making process, increasingly acquiring legislative, supervisory and budgetary responsibilities, but this is not enough to complete a process of democratisation towards a European parliamentary democracy and, in this way, bring citizens closer to supranational policy decisions[24]. The truth is that, despite the growth of powers, the EP must continue to struggle to assert its role and defend its powers, which it does with difficulty but often successfully through various tactical approaches[25]. In all this the role of the administration (i.e., Civil Servants and administrative organisation) is recognised to be decisive thanks to the action and skills of the staff[26].

But it does not end there: in a world[27] (not just in Europe) where the (growing) phenomena of regression of democratic systems concern important countries, the focus falls on the role of public administration.[28] In fact, the new regimes, geared towards illiberal or authori-

---

[23]From the Outline Presentation of the conference *40 Years etc. cit.*

[24]In the introduction of the EP document *Towards direct elections etc. cit.* it says that the EP "has always understood its role as the voice of the citizens, strongly defending their interests".

[25]The entire keynote speech of Professor Adrienne Héritier at the conference *40 Years etc. cit.,* was dedicated to this central issue: first move, consultation, invoking ECJ, delaying decisions, alliance with other actors, de facto pressures and so on, are among the instruments used by the EP. See A. Héritier & al., *European Parliament ascendant: parliamentary strategies of self-empowerment in the EU,* Palgrave Macmillan, London, 2019.

[26]A specific report on this issue was presented at the *40 Years etc. cit.* conference by Professor Ch. Neuhold: the EP staff acts by offering knowledge and advice in very different fields, holding politicised competences, drawing up drafts, ensuring (steering role) policies run and so on.

[27]AA.VV. *La grande regressione. Quindici intellettuali da tutto il mondo spiegano la crisi del nostro tempo,* a cura di Heinrich Geiselbergern, Feltrinelli, Milano, 2017.

[28]In an international symposium at the highest level, organised in Fiesole 31 January – 1 February, EUI Workshop on *Democratic Backsliding and Public Administration* it was decided to concentrate the analysis on this issue. I have been requested to make a report on *How the EU deals with democratic backsliding in member states.*

tarian orientations, firstly try to make the public administration their own instrument so as to implement their policy: this is a crucial step. The administration's reaction, its resilience and its evolution is decisive in the future of democracy.[29] Just to be clear: this is not a political opinion, this a legal duty because Democracy is a fundamental value of the European Union: the articles of the Treaty that form the base of the defence, development and promotion of the EU's fundamental values are art. 2[30], art. 3 e 13 (which guarantee their protection both within the Union and with third-party countries), Art. 7 (which provides for a procedure against Member States that attack these essential values). We must also remember that Art. 49 requires respect for essential values as a condition for EU membership. The EU is therefore committed to the achievement, defence and promotion of Democracy as a fundamental value.

In short, here is what can be deduced from all the previous observations: democracy defends itself at supranational level, in the European Union, and is transformed thanks to technology. In our age, we are witnessing on the one hand increasingly widespread phenomena of regression of democratic systems under the pressure of modern authoritarian approaches, and on the other a challenge to the functioning of institutions under the pressure of the use of new technologies[31].

---

[29] Among the many valid contributions, I would like to point out in particular a preparatory report by M. W. Bauer, *Understanding the Anti-Pluralist Challenge for the Democratic Administration*, Fiesole, 27 November, 2018 (typewritten).

[30] Article 2 TEU: The Union is founded on the values of respect for human dignity, freedom, **democracy**, equality, the rule of law and respect for human rights, including the rights of persons belonging to minorities. These values are common to the Member States in a society in which pluralism, non-discrimination, tolerance, justice, solidarity and equality between women and men prevail.

[31] I dealt with the two themes both at operational level (as a European official for thirty years) and at academic level (I taught these subjects at the universities of Milan and Ancona), and I proposed two distinct theoretical contributions in the books *Being European* and *E - Democracy* already mentioned above. In truth, I realised that the two themes, European dimension and technological impact, are closely linked and should not be separated when reflecting on the future of democracy: the awareness of the strong connection of the two aspects matured in me during my fellowship at the European University Institute of Florence (of which this study is the result), which enriched my knowledge and my reflection in

We have also seen that in order to provide good answers we must have correct communication in place[32], which faces up to obstacles like lack of information on the mechanisms and functions of the European Union, the imbalance that has favoured the weight of states (national governments) and the failure to concentrate communication (at all levels) on the policies of the European Union[33]. This has hindered the promotion of the "awareness" of citizens on the role (also worldwide) of the Union. These topics of communication, information and public awareness have been very focused during the period that preceded the 2019 European elections. The EP administration made an exceptional effort, crowned with success, but also other actors have engaged in this proactive campaign. Among them there is also the European University Institute. The EUI organised, just ahead of the elections, a study day entitled "European elections: what does it matter?" And I was invited on to the opening panel[34]. On that occasion, we were asked various simple and direct questions, and for this very reason interesting: the first of the questions was "why do we care about the European elections?" To answer the question, I began by denouncing a paradox: the fiercest criticisms and accusations made of the European Union concern issues and sectors that are not a

---

an extraordinary way, completing what has already been developed in Milan and Ancona.

[32] An excellent event on this issue has been organised by EUI School of Transnational Governance, on 1-2 April 2019 in Florence: *Communicating Europe*. The keynote speaker was Jaume Duch (*The Power of Communication*), who stressed, inter alia, that politics does not exist without communication, that a competition exists between national and European level in communicating, that we need to build a European public opinion and create trust. They are all important elements for a "correct" communication. In this event, I held a workshop on *The impact of technology on Democracy*.

[33] A very personal feeling, nothing more than a feeling (hence why only in the footnote): Sometimes I get the impression that in analysing the situation, some would like or imagine an EU alone and by itself, with the other actors as an annoying element that one would gladly do without, actors who dare to try to be better than the EU. Well, the world is not like that, on the contrary it becomes more and more multipolar: if anything, the problem is the opposite, and it is to understand if the EU will be able to be one of these poles.

[34] The event, organised as part of the Festival d'Europa, took place in Florence on 12 May 2019. In addition to the initial roundtable, seminars were held on various topics, before the conclusions of EUI president prof. R. Dehousse.

part of its direct competence: immigration, foreign policy, terrorism, even regional nationalism and so on. Why does this happen? What happens? The European Union is (thanks to the European Council, which has become an institution) the place where today the Member States try to find an agreement on the big problems, even beyond the competences properly called the Union. Which, in itself, is positive. The fact is that when agreement is not found (which is often) it is a failure of the states, but it appears or is passed on as a failure of the Union, maliciously defined with the generic term 'Europe'. A split Europe, which does not decide, detached and so on, are the most common epithets. So: why do I care about the European elections? I care, I replied, that the European Union can take decisions at supranational level even in these sectors, which today are not within its competence. On the other hand, we never talk about the great achievements made by the European Union in the sectors that are its responsibility: if we take the environment, consumers, transport, free movement, the economy, the great progress made by the Union have made my life (not ten or a hundred but) a thousand times better than when I was a child and a teenager.

This is not talked about and I care, I added, that the EU continues to take care of and regulate these sectors. I then concluded by saying that I really care that this peaceful space that is the European Union continues to exist, of which the European Parliament is a pillar that we must continue to consolidate, also with the contribution of its administration.

Closing

At this point, it seems that the best way to end this exercise is to remember what was said by one of the most important classical authors, J.M. Keynes, in a conference held in 1921 (almost a century ago), talking about the Civil Service. Keynes praised fundamental characteristics like independence, quality, detachment, wisdom and prestige that ensure that the institution for which one works is respected.[35] Such recognition of the delicate importance of the role of the public administration confirms the validity of the decision to consecrate time and energy to the elaboration of this study. Indeed, I frankly believe that this can also be said of the staff of the European Parliament. But I also believe that all these characteristics are not simply acquired once and then automatically remain: we must always look for the working methods that favour them, like the EPA has done all these years. I hope that, perhaps, this study has made a small contribution in this direction.

---

[35] J.M. Keynes, *Il Tesoro*, FULM edition, Rome, 2018. Keynes' writings focus on the administration of the British Treasury (for which he worked) but also contains considerations of a more general significance.

References

R. Dehousse, *The Euro Crisis and Beyond: The Transformation of the European Political System*, RSCAS 2018/67 Robert Schuman Centre for Advanced Studies, December 2018

M. Piantini, *La parabola d'Europa*, Donzelli Editore, Roma, 2019

Jean Monnet, *Mémoires*, Fayard, Paris, 1976

I. Kershaw, *Roller coaster: Europe 1950-2017*, Penguin UK, London, 2018.

F. Fukuyama, *Identity. The Demand for Dignity and the Politics of Resentment*, Edition Farrar Straus and Giroux, New York, 2018.

Daniel Innerarity, *La Democracia en Europa*, Galaxia Gutenberg SL, Barcelona, 2017.

H. Arendt, *Truth and Politics*, in The New Yorker, February 25, 1967

N. Lupo - A. Manzella, *Il Parlamento europeo. Una introduzione*, Luiss University Press, Roma, 2019.

Ch. Verger (rapporteur), *Le Parlement européen un parlement différent*, Décryptage, 3 May 2019, Notre Europe, Paris.

M. Telò, *Les élections européennes: le risque de "muddling through"*, in Actualité Carte blanche, IEE, Brussels, 28 May 2019.

I. Ortenzi, *Innovation manager*, Franco Angeli Editore, Milano, 2018

M. Morgan, R.E. Levitt, W. Malek, *Executing your strategy*, Boston, Harvard Business School Press, 2007

World Bank 2019 World Development Report "The Changing Nature of Work", Washington, 2019.

F. Caselli, *Technology differences over space and time*, Princeton University Press, Oxford, 2017

S. Allcorn and H.F. Stein, *The Dysfunctional Workplace. Theory, Stories and Practices*, University of Missouri Press, Columbia, 2015

M. Wolf, *Lettore vieni a casa. Il cervello che legge in un mondo digitale*, Edizioni Vita e Pensiero, Milano, 2018.

M. Garcia, N. de Peganow, *Innovation participative*, Édition Scrineo, Paris 2012

J. Fox, *Comment être un bon manager*, Archipoche, Paris 2004

D.W. Bijl, *The New Way of Working*, PARCC, Zeewolde 2011

C. Pollitt – G. Bouckaert, *Public Management Reform. A Comparative Analysis*, Oxford, Oxford University Press, 2011

R. Maconick – P. Morgan, *Capacity-building supported by the United Nations* United Nations Editions, 1999

A. De Waal, *The Secret of High performance Organizations*, Management Online Review, April, 2010

B.G. Dale – T. van der Wiele – T. van Iwaarden, *Managing Quality*, Wiley-Blackwell, Oxford, 2007

European Commission, *Quality of Public Administration. A Toolbox for practitioners*, Luxembourg, European Union, 2015

European Ombudsman *The European Code of Good Administrative Behaviour*, European Unions, Strasbourg, 2013.

J. Beckford, *The Intelligent Organization*, Routledge, London, 2016

Frances Frei *(Harvard Business School), How to build (and rebuild) trust*, Ted Talk, 4 May 2018 (YouTube)

E. Laurent, *L'impasse collaborative*, Les liens qui libèrent, Paris, 2018

M. Benedick – R. Collart, *Bâtir une organisation collaborative*, Pearson France, Montreuil, 2018

G. Bouckaert – J. Halligan, *Managing Performance: International Comparison*, Routledge, London, 2008

A. Maccaferri, *L'empatia degli spazi accresce produttività e qualità della vita*, in Domenica 24-Ore 18 Novembre 2018

A. Monica – G. Balduzzi (ed.), *Governare il cambiamento istituzionale e organizzativo nelle amministrazioni europee*, Pavia University Press, Pavia, 2019

G. Della Cananea – D.U. Galetta (a cura di), *Codice ReNEUAL del procedimento amministrativo dell'Unione europea*, Editoriale Scientifica, Napoli, 2016.

A. Baricco, *The Game*, Einaudi, Torino, 2018.

Interview of Daniele Novara (by M. Croci), in Sette - Corriere della Sera on 6 December 2018.

A. Héritier & al., *European Parliament ascendant: parliamentary strategies of self-empowerment in the EU*, Palgrave Macmillan, London, 2019

AA.VV. *La grande regressione. Quindici intellettuali da tutto il mondo spiegano la crisi del nostro tempo*, a cura di Heinrich Geiselbergern Feltrinelli, Milano, 2017.

J.M. Keynes, *Il Tesoro*, FULM edition, Rome, 2018

http://tuned-arch.it/home.html

https://www.danpontefract.com/learning-by-osmosis/tuned-arch.it/home.html (Dan Pontefract, *Learning by osmosis*)

https://www.managementstudyguide.com/
importance-of-vision-and-mission-statements.htm

https://www.cornerstonedynamics.com/
3-big-benefits-of-a-clear-vision-statement/

https://www.envisio.com/blog/benefits-of-strategic-planning

https://bustin.com/executive-leadership-blog/why_bother_10_
benefits_of_planning/

https://www.cliffsnotes.com/study-guides/
principles-of-management

https://www.managementstudyguide.com/planning_advantages.
htm

https://www.denizon.com/operational...
/matrix-management-benefits-and-pitfalls/

https://www.management-square.com/matrix-organization/

https://www.referenceforbusiness.com/encyclopedia/Man-Mix/
Matrix-Management-and-Structure.html

https://www.managementstudyguide.com/what-are-metrics.htm

https://www.linkedin.com/pulse/benefits-having-right-kpis-key-
performance-indicators-stephen-lynch

https://www.isixsigma.com/implementation/basics/
importance-implementing-effective-metrics/

G. Vilella, *Being European*, Nomos Verlag, Baden Baden, 2017

G. Vilella, *E-Democracy*, Nomos Verlag, Baden-Baden, 2019.

SEMINARS AND WORKSHOPS

5 September 2018: ECJ former President V. Skouris on "*Leaders beyond the State*", focused on the negative sentiments against Europe today, EUI, Florence.

18 September 2018: prof. Koops on "*Digital investigations and New Privacy*", focused on the role of technologies in the Criminal Law, EUI, Florence.

26 September 2018: prof. Marise Cremona on "*The EU as an international actor*", focused on the legal basis and legal scrutiny of the external activities, EUI, Florence.

10 October 2018: Reading Group on "*lying in politics, post-truth politics, and fake news*" (EUI Fellows, Florence).

10 October 2018: M.Galeotti-D.Toshkov-O.Westerwinter: "*Challenges to Governance beyond the State*", EUI, Florence.

11 October 2018: International Conference on "*Law via Intranet*", University of Florence.

16 October 2018: "*Legislative Transparency in the EU: what can happen after the recent Luxembourg Jurisprudence*" (E. De Capitani), EUI, Florence.

18 October 2018: Policy Dialogue – *European Parliamentary Elections: Challenges and Opportunities of New Digital Technologies*, EUI Florence and EP Brussels.

19 ottobre 2018: Joint European University Institute/College of Europe Conference, *The Impact of Populism on EU polity and policies*, EUI, Florence.

22 October 2018: Università Statale di Milano, Lectio magistralis by European University Institute's Secretary General, Vincenzo Grassi, on "*La crisi del sentimento europeista: cause, origini e prospettive*"

8 November 2018.: F. Pizzetti, *GDPR, codice italiano e Data Protection Officer*, conference held at the Università Politecnica delle Marche, Ancona.

19 November 2018: Conference by EP Vicepresident D.M. Sassoli, on "*La necessità di una corretta comunicazione in vista delle elezioni europee*" European University Institute, Florence.

22 - 23 of November 2018: Conference *40 Years of European Parliament Direct Elections*, held at the European University Institute, Florence.

6 December 2018: Max Weber Lecture *"When Sovereigns Stir"*, held by professor N. Walker, EUI, Florence.

23 January 2019: *Migration, Globalisation and the Nation*, speaker prof. A. Triandafyllidou, EUI, Florence.

24 January 2019: *Integrating Difference in the European Union (InDivEU)*. The kick-off meeting of the H2020 project, EUI, Florence.

25 January 2019: Workshop *E-Democracy*, with EP Vice-President Fabio Massimo Castaldo and high level panel: B. Laffan, G. Umbach, D.U. Galetta, L. Orgad, T. Karapiperis.I had the honour to make the keynote speech, EUI, Florence.

28 January 2019: *Roundtable: "Towards a Cyber Union? The EU's added value in managing complexity in cyberspace"*, EUI, Florence.

29 January 2019: Seminar *The EP Behind the Scenes: A Discussion with Jean-Paul Denanot*, EUI, Florence.

31 January- 1 February, EUI Workshop on *Democratic Backsliding and Public Administration*, EUI, Florence.

20 March 2019: Max Weber Lecture *"Advanced Capitalism, Advanced Democracies and National Autonomy: Symbiotic Most of Time"*, Prof. David Soskice, EUI, Florence.

1-2 April 2019: *Communicating Europe* (Executive Training Seminar: J. Duch keynote speaker), EUI School of Transnational Governance, Florence.

4 April 2019: Roundtable, *World Bank 2019 World Development Report "The Changing Nature of Work"*, EUI, Florence.

2-3 May 2019 *The State of the Union*, EUI, Florence:
- European Parliament's diplomacy in support of Democracy in the EU's Eastern Neighbourhood (Workshop)
- Do we really need politicians? E-Democracy vs. representative democracy (Roundtable)
- Il futuro della democrazia (Tavola Rotonda)
- Defending Democracy against Disinformation and Cyber-threats (Special Roundtable)

7 May 2019: *Stato e Amministrazione di fronte alla rivoluzione delle ICT: partecipazione, diritti e nuovi attori*, Milan (Università Statale)

9 May 2019: *Governare il cambiamento istituzionale e organizzativo nelle amministrazioni europee*, Milan (Università Statale)

12 May 2019: *Festival d'Europa* (EUI, Florence)
- Elezioni europee che ci importa?

EP DOCUMENTS

Report to the President. Implementation of the Administrative Work Programme 2009-2011, Brussels, December 2011

The European Parliament 2025 - Preparing for complexity, Brussels, January 2012

MEP 2025 - Preparing the Future Work Environment for Members of the European Parliament Brussels, March 2012 (Vice-president responsible: R. Wieland)

CSG EP 2025 Team, *Preparing for complexity*, Brussels March, 2013 (Responsible for EP 2025 process: F. Debié)

K. Welle, *Preparing for complexity - Final Report*, April 2013

Stock-taking of the internal rules and administrative procedures applied in the European Parliament: conclusions of the Administrative Task Force on Simplification, Brussels 16 December 2013 (Vice-president responsible: D. Roth-Behrendt)

Administrative Work Programme. January 2014 update (Brussels)

The Secretary General, *Parliamentary Project Portfolio within the Strategic Execution Framework of the European Parliament*, Brussels, October 2014

K. Welle (editor), *One Hundred Steps Forward: The European Parliament and the Upgrading of European Democracy since the Lisbon Treaty*, Brussels, April 2014

Fact Sheets, Bruxelles-Luxembourg, 2017

Rolling legislative agenda of the European Union Brussels, September 2014, prepared by the director-generals for internal policies, R. Ribera d'Alcalà, and external policies, M.Aguiriano Nalda, together with the Secretary-General.

Strategic Agenda for the Union in Times of Changes Statement by the European Council at the meeting on 27 June 2014

J. Dunne, *Mapping the Cost of Non-Europe 2014-2019*, Brussels, April 2015, preceded by two now-updated versions

The Secretary General, *Strategic Execution Framework 2017-2019 for the Administration of the European Parliament*, 13 January 2017 (Away Day Final)

K. Welle (editor), *Strategic Execution Framework for the Administration of the European Parliament 2017-2019*, Brussels, December 2017 (Responsible staff: F. Debié, A. Cabanelas, F. Renuit, S. Rogowski)

Strategic Execution Framework, Brussels, European Parliament, December 2018 (Responsible: F. Debié)

Ideas Papers for the Innovation Day 2019 , Twelve ideas papers produced by the European Parliamentary Research Service (s.d. s.l., however it is Brussels December 2018)

Strategic Execution Framework 2019-2021. Directorates-General, Brussels, April 2019

3rd Management Innovation Day. Contributions of the Directorates-General to the SEF 2019-2021 (K. Welle editor), Brussels, April, 2019

Europe's two trillion euro dividend. Mapping the Cost of Non-Europe, 2019-24 (A. Teasdale editor), Brussels, April 2019

Innovative Working in the European Parliament. A guide, Brussels, November 2016

E. Gebhardt, *Foreword to Technological Innovation and democracy*, Brussels, May 2017

EP Resolution P8_TA(2017)095, 16 March 2017, on "E-Democracy in the EU: potential and challanges".

H. Kerzner, *Project Management, Metrics, KPIs and Dashboards. A Guide to Measuring and Monitoring Project Performance*, Wiley New York, 2017

C. Pennell, *Maturity in Government Digital Transformation Journeys*, September 2018

L. Délépine et al., *IT Governance Hub*, Brussels, August, 2018

EPRS, Historical Archives Unit, *40th Anniversary of the 1976 Act on Direct Elections to the European Parliament*, EU Luxembourg, 2015

CARDOC, DG PRES, *Towards direct elections to the European Parliament*, European Communities, Luxembourg, 2009

CSG, Building continent-wide democracy, Responsible administrator: F. Debié, December, 2012

The Secretary General, *Parliamentary democracy in action: summary*, March 2013

ITEC, *EP Technology Clock 2019*, 24 April 2018

ITEC, *EU Tech Study Tour*, Final Report, February 2018

Photo Credits

www.ingramcontent.com/pod-product-compliance
Lightning Source LLC
LaVergne TN
LVHW091525170726
843492LV00004B/1066